The Way Of Coffee

How Coffee Transformed The World, Promotes Happiness And Protects Against Disease

Chris Kilham

Medicine Hunter

Contents

Dedication

To Zoe, with love, and to many more steaming cups

Gratitude

Many people have helped one way or another with this book. Special thanks to Olivier Fahy at Berkem, who has provided valuable support for the completion of this work. I am deeply grateful for that.

Thanks also to George Howell and The Coffee Connection, Dave Copeland and River Road Coffee, Jacques Dikansky, Thierry Lambert, Benoit Lemaire, Zachary and Johanna Gibson, Russell and Mickey Archibald, the people at Greenwell, K.C. Miller, Jean Paul Coupal, Craig Weatherby, Travis Hammond, Sergio Cam, the people at La Florida, Mario at Shambari Campa, Edouard Fleury, Axel d'Hauthuille, Fredericke Wong, Jerome Lippens, Congo crew Anant, Brieuc, Francois, Jean, pilots Paul and Jeff, Nebil Bourguiba, Ben and Edison at Helena Coffee, Trung Nguyen Coffee Village, Nescafe' WASI Coffee Farm Experience Center, World Coffee Museum, Aaron Davis at Kew, Dean Draznin, Linda Sparrow, Zoe Helene and the multitude of good people who have cheered me on with this project. This would never have happened without all of your kind support and encouragement.

Chris Kilham

Western Massachusetts 2025

About the Author

Chris Kilham is a medicine hunter, author, educator, and yogi. Chris conducts medicinal plant research and sustainable botanical sourcing all over the globe, helping companies to develop and popularize traditional plant-based food and medicinal products into market successes. He works to bridge worlds, regularly sharing information about other cultures through presentations and media.

Chris has appeared on hundreds of radio and TV programs worldwide and is the author of sixteen books. In the course of this work, Chris has traveled millions of miles and has spent thousands of days and nights away from home. He has fire-walked in the South Pacific, been made a chief, enjoyed a consular post for three years, has made good friends all over the globe, roamed remote rainforests and mountains, engaged in ceremonial journeys with shamans, and explored wild places, from deserts to rivers.

The New York Times called Chris "part David Attenborough, part Indiana Jones." An avid body surfer and ardent traveler, Chris lives with his wife, cultural activist Zoe Helene, in western Massachusetts. His motto is "go big or go home."

Chapter 1
An Intimate Connection

Introduction

In the beginning was the word, and the word was coffee. And the heavens opened up, and from the sovereign realms of majesty and grace, humanity was granted a gift of a tree. And this tree bore fruit. And this fruit bore seeds. And those seeds, when roasted in hot iron over open flames, rendered a dark bean which, when crushed and boiled in water and drunk piping hot, emboldened humanity, flinging wide open the rusty doors of perception, and causing people to commit great works. And this divine potation shook the shoulders of the world, and set in motion a vast and brilliant conversation that would never end. And lo, the history of the ages was transformed as a result. Coffee, mighty coffee, regal coffee, coffee the divine, coffee the marvelous, coffee the greatest of all, has given to us brilliance and wit and joy and pleasure!

Coffee arabica Kohler's Medicinal Plants

1

Have you ever stopped to ask yourself what our relationship is with plants? We eat them, we drink their juices, we breathe their air, we wear their fibers, we build homes made of them, we burn them for fuel, we adorn ourselves and our environments with their blossoms, we dab ourselves with their fragrances and oils, and we utilize them as the most widely employed medicines on earth. Our lives are inextricably intertwined with plants. Plants remarkably take in carbon dioxide and give off oxygen, and that air keeps us alive. Trees and shrubs shade us against a hot sun. Plants fertilize the soil. Plants inspire us. Without plants, we could not live. In the mad rush to pave and build on every last square inch of our fair planet, we forget that we must keep lots of space for plants. Otherwise, we will remove ourselves and life in general from the planetary equation.

It is with this broad understanding of our intimate relationship with plants that we can consider coffee, a once obscure Abyssinian tree that now dominates agriculture in the tropical and sub-tropical world, and whose products can be found in homes from as far afield from one another as Los Angeles and Kathmandu, Rio and London, Geneva and Moscow, Adelaide and Anchorage. Just as plants loom large in our lives, coffee looms large in the human diet and culture.

"Oh coffee, thou dost disperse cares and sorrow, thou art the drink of the friends of God, thou givest health to those who labor to obtain wisdom."

- Sheikh Abd al-Kadir

I am convinced that Hell is not as Dante depicted, all fire and torment with helpless souls chained to walls, wailing in agony. No, hell is a place of eternal dullness, devoid of sense or sensation, a joyless realm of complete indifference. There, the coffee is execrable. Harsh beans, poorly roasted, are ground too coarse and extracted too sparingly, producing a thin, brown water which burns for hours on a Bunn O Matic until the vapors smell like a soiled scrub sponge that has been kept damp in a dark sink cabinet. In Hell, the coffee is lousy. In Hell, there is no reverie.

In Cambridge, Massachusetts, the very best cup of coffee was served for many years at The Coffee Connection. That was before proprietor George Howell, who fussed over his coffee like precious gems in a jeweler's display window, sold out to coffee giant Starbucks.

Frankly, I do not know how The Coffee Connection did it. The coffee was impenetrably dark, the aroma seductive, the taste knee-buckling marvelous. Their shop in Harvard Square was my second office, and there I conducted business for many years over steaming French presses of the finest coffees in the world.

Angels arose heavenward from the cup, the purfled purple clouds of dawn parted to reveal a splendid, beaming sun, and shiny brass trumpets pointed to the sparkling skies, declaring the brilliance of the day with regal fanfare. Not The Four Seasons, nor Starbucks, nor Peets can conjure such a cup. Perhaps George Howell made a pact with the Devil. It is not my problem. The coffee was that good.

Thankfully, Howell returned to his beans at the end of his non-compete with Starbucks, and may we thank our lucky stars for that. His three Greater Boston area George Howell Coffee locations serve the rare and gorgeous and swooning delicious coffees of the old Coffee Connection, plus scads of others from fincas large and small, far and wide. Those who by fate or fortune work or live nearby are blessed with ready access to some of the greatest coffee on Earth. I would go as far as to say that in all the world, for the millions of miles I have traveled, the countless cafes I have visited and thousands of cups of coffee I have drunk, Howell's holds an honored place in the coffee empyrean. Way to go, George.

We are built for pleasure. Every sense we possess has the capacity for delight, for rich enjoyment. We are meant to relish and savor, through sight, sound, touch, smell, taste and thought. Our brains secrete ingenious pleasure chemicals, in which our otherwise dull gray cells bathe as if in a broth of nectar.

A rich aromatic cup of coffee, brewed lovingly and drunk thoughtfully, delights the mind and banishes fatigue. It flings the eyes open, like a window thrown up to the sensual delights of a spring day. If you don't care for coffee, then by all means don't touch it. But if you enjoy coffee, then sip and savor without guilt or concern. Coffee is *good* for you, *good* for you, *good* for you, as you shall discover. Coffee is a wonderful thing, a gift from the gods, to relieve the fatigue of weary humanity. Coffee inspires.

Humans love coffee; there is no doubt about that. Few things we put into our mouths provide such an instantaneous effect, one that people quickly come to enjoy. The simple coffee bean has become a global colossus, a widely traded commodity sold all over the world. After water, coffee is the most widely consumed beverage, surpassing tea, sodas, juices, and alcoholic beverages. Over 2.25 billion cups of coffee are consumed every day, providing energy, alertness, and a host of significant health benefits to be described in significant detail later on. Coffee is a start to the day for billions of people, the clarion call in a cup that stirs us to wakefulness and propels us into our busy lives. It is an agent of conversation, a starter of meetings, a welcome pause in an overly long day, a soothing respite after hours, a steaming brew over which one can share confidences.

Since its discovery and popularization, coffee has had an immense impact on humanity, functioning simultaneously as a stimulant, an agent of conversation, a colossus of international commerce, a source of great pleasure, and a beneficial plant with the capacity to ameliorate some of the most pernicious health disturbances of our time. Yes, friends, coffee is a preventive medicine.

"Coffee, the sober drink, the mighty nourishment of the brain, which, unlike other spirits, heightens purity and lucidity; coffee, which clears the clouds of the imagination and their gloomy weight; which illumines the reality of things suddenly with the flash of truth..."

- 1600s description of coffee

My day consistently begins with coffee. Even when traveling to remote places, my Aero Press and freshly ground organic city roast coffee are always in my bag. Coffee preparation is a task I approach with meticulous care and attention to the ensuing potation and the illuminating reverie it promotes.

At home, I am typically up in the fives, but my wife Zoe slumbers on for hours more. Following a shower, I proceed into the kitchen to my coffee maker. I have, by fastidious trial, determined the exact measure of whole beans to make a large cup of rich, bold, fragrant coffee. I want a bracing cup of coffee that will grab me by the shoulders, stand me up straight, and give me the power to march through a busy day.

Though many single varieties of coffee are delicious, I prefer to craft my own blend. Most of the time, I mix even parts dark-roasted Sumatran, Ethiopian Yirgacheffe, and Balinese varieties. The result is a strong, rich brew with deep and complex flavor notes. The coffee at home is always organically grown, whole bean, without toxic agricultural chemicals.

The grinding makes a clatter, but still I hear no stirring from the bedroom. I patiently place the fine grind into a paper filter (unbleached always, no dioxin), and pour with exacting care freshly boiled spring water.

The pouring process must be accomplished in such a manner that the water comes in contact with all the ground coffee evenly, ensuring the strongest possible brew. I take my time, pouring a bit of water and allowing that to filter down, and then doing so several times more.

If you bring Zen-like precision to the making of coffee, it will deliver great satisfaction. Practice yields superb coffee, and that is well worth the practice.

"The morning cup of coffee has an exhilaration about it which the cheering influence of the afternoon or evening cup of tea cannot be expected to reproduce."

~Oliver Wendell Holmes, Sr.

When coffee is made and I am assured of a fragrant and lively brew that will embolden the spirit, rally the mind like a brace of coronets, and open the eyes wide to the clear beaming light of day, then I sit on the Persian rug in the living room, sipping slowly.

The aromatic vapors of a perfect cup lead the mind to wakefulness by the nose, while the precious caffeine in the brew opens the body's energetic floodgates. Coffee wipes clean the windows of perception to sparkling, glassy brilliance. Hundreds of beneficial biologically active compounds, a veritable battalion of healthy phytochemicals, charge like the Light Brigade into the body and rush to every organ system.

Sometime later on, once the sun is fully risen, after the various rabbits, squirrels, and chipmunks have frolicked in our yard for a good long time, Zoe rises. I fastidiously repeat the coffee-making process for her, and when she emerges from her morning shower, a steaming cup awaits her on the kitchen counter.

When I travel on my own and call home, Zoe tells me in a somewhat dejected tone that the coffee she makes isn't as good as mine. I insist that it's because I possess special coffee mojo. In actuality, the case is that I have figured out a formula, and meticulously engaged to produce a delightful cup.

"The first coffee links me with a world I love in an almost secret way."

- Colette Modiano

According to aggregated trade figures from numerous organizations, approximately 125 million people depend on coffee agriculture to live.

As many as 800 million people in the world work with coffee in some manner. Global production of coffee in exporting countries for the year 2022/2023 was a staggering 178,000,000 bags. With the standard trade weight of a bag of coffee at 60 kilos or approximately 132 pounds, that adds up to an enormous 11,748,000 tons or 23,496,000,000 (more than 23 billion) pounds. That's a whopping load of coffee. Brazil is far and away the world's leading grower and exporter of coffee, producing 63,300,000 bags of coffee in 2022/2023. You can think of Brazil as a brawny titan of coffee commerce, a caffeinated Goliath, whose massive coffee production exceeds by more than double that of the country in the number two slot, the Southeast Asian nation of Vietnam (26,300,000 bags).

In third and fourth places, Colombia (12,400,000 bags) and Indonesia (10,900,000 bags) weigh in respectively. Production and export of coffee from 50 nations is monitored monthly by various trade organizations and departments of agriculture. If you wish to take a deep dive into coffee information, see the International Coffee Organization website, which details just about everything coffee.

Those of us who work with botanicals of various types, including herbs, spices, coffee, tea, cacao, and medicinal plants, often feel called by the plants. There is an insistent tug at the corners of the mind, an urge to go find out more. Over the course of several decades, I have felt the ineluctable pull of many plants, including kava, maca, ginseng, rhodiola, ashwagandha, tea, cacao, and coffee. In the case of coffee, I have chased the tree and its fruit and its resulting beverage all over the tropics.

Coffee's effect on humanity is breathtaking. This astonishing tree, whose fruits yield a seed that has changed the course of history, has its own gravitational pull. I have been drawn into its orbit, investigating it in the tropics along the coffee belt and drinking its seemingly innumerable preparations. I have been inspired by coffee, energized by coffee, and brought to foreign lands and marvelous people thanks to coffee. In many ways, coffee has greatly enriched my life. *The Way of Coffee* is my humble offering in return. Please come along on the ride.

Vintage Coffee Sign

Chapter 2
A First Sighting 1995

In my line of work, investigating medicinal and beneficial plants of all kinds, first sightings stand out as special moments. I think back with great fondness to my first tea plantation in the Nilgiri Hills of India, first cocoa plantation in Central America, first farm of golden raspberries in Siberia, and first ginseng plantation in far northeastern China. The sight of healthy plants glistening in the sun fills me with a sense of wonder.

Many people who work with plants have the experience of being drawn to the plants, as though these clever agents of nature have figured out ways to woo and lure us in. It is certainly the case for me with coffee.

The simple beans of the coffee tree have altered human history, changed the course of world events, and today fuel hundreds of millions of people every day. And they have definitely wooed me to them. I am often asked what my favorite herb or medicinal plant is.

These days, I simply say coffee, which surprises most people. But when I review in my mind the frequency of my coffee consumption (daily), the amount of coffee I typically consume (about a liter a day), the innumerable verified benefits of consuming coffee, and my deep investigations in the field and in the library, coffee is without doubt my number one favorite.

Even today, decades after the fact, I can still vividly recall my first sighting of coffee growing. A brilliant golden sun rose up in the early morning sky as I wandered a quiet dirt lane in the hills above San Juan, Costa Rica, winding in a serpentine design up along a sloping mountain.

After a mile or so of walking, I chanced upon a small jewel of a coffee plantation, not more than a couple of acres, with exquisitely manicured and tended coffee trees. Whoever managed that little plantation took great care; everything was in its place and well cared-for.

A neat netted garden shed housed the tools that kept the several hundred coffee trees expertly tended. I wandered delighted through the rows. Each tree stood about two meters high. The bright, waxy, spear-shaped leaves of the coffee trees shone a dark green. On slender branches adorned by fragrant white blossoms, clusters of ripe red coffee cherries hung heavily. I picked one and popped it into my mouth, and bit into the thin skin and pulp of the cherry.

The two beans inside, covered with a sweet mucilage, slipped easily out of the skin, which I spat out. I sucked on the mucilage surrounding the beans, taking in a delicate floral sweetness. When the sweetness was all gone, I spat out the beans, picked another cherry, and started over. There was no one else around.

The year-round temperature of that area, between 20 – 25 °C, combined with volcanic soil, almost daily rainfall, and an elevation of about 1000 feet, added up to perfect growing conditions for the coffee trees I was observing, and for others throughout Costa Rica. Hundreds of Costa Rican coffee farms called *fincas*, many of them modest in size, produce top-quality arabica coffee beans with excellent flavor and aroma. I had drunk some excellent coffee during my stay in Costa Rica, whose coffee is known for its fine flavor. But this was the first time I had ever stood in a coffee orchard, the first time I had ever picked a ripe coffee cherry, the first time I ever saw for myself the slender, beautiful trees which produce one of the most gigantic commodities in the world.

On tree branches overhead, gaily-colored songbirds warbled and sang. The sun felt warm on my neck. I broke naturally into a broad smile, recalling a proclamation made by the famous physician William Harvey that "This little fruit is the source of happiness and wit!" He could also have added that the coffee tree is beautiful to behold, a graceful work of nature which delights the eye as much as its fruits stimulate body and mind. Since then, I have walked among many coffee plantations. But I have never forgotten my first time.

Chapter 3
A Case of Frisky Goats

Those plants that demonstrate the highest value in cultures and those that play central roles in societies often have legends concerning their origins. In the case of coffee, the legend concerns livestock - goats, to be exact. And from there flows one of the greatest histories of any plant ever embraced by humans.

Stories repeated often enough become part of history, and this is the case with coffee. The discovery of coffee and its invigorating properties traces back to humble surroundings and a simple man, according to improbable circumstances concerning a group of goats. Whether the tale is true or apocryphal, I cannot say, but it has become intrinsic to coffee's legend.

According to folklore, sometime around 800 in the fertile hills of East Africa's Kingdom of Axum, which is now known as Ethiopia, a goat herd named Kaldi was tending his flock.

One day, as he was enjoying a rest in the warm sun, Kaldi observed his goats unusually lively and rambunctious. They danced and jumped and gamboled. The goat herd was curious at this and paid close attention to the behavior of the frisky flock. He noticed that after eating the berries of a small tree, the goats became animated.

Kaldi tried eating some of the berries, and he too soon felt a peculiar invigoration. He brought some of the berries to the village where he lived, and his neighbors also tested the enlivening properties of the new berries.

The people in that region made a tea-like beverage brewed from the hard green beans inside the berries. They called the tree that bore the berries *kaffa*, and the beverage made from its berries was named *kaffa* as well. Little did they know that this was the beginning of a global revolution. Today, Ethiopian coffee varieties, notably Harrar and Yirgacheffe, are regarded as among the finest coffees in the world.

"No matter what historians claimed, BC really stood for 'Before Coffee."

— Cherise Sinclair, *Master of the Mountain*

A couple of hundred years later, across the Gulf of Barbera in the sparse and rugged foothills of the Yemen countryside, adjacent to the Arabian Sea, yet another poor goatherd tended a flock belonging to the fabled Shehodet Mosque, whose faithful devoted their minds and hearts to the worship of mighty Allah, may his name be praised.

The goats provided the company of the pious with a steady supply of milk, butter, meat, and leather. The goatherds of the mosque, in turn, treated the animals with care, allowing them freedom to roam, climb, and frolic. By day, the goats nibbled on short grasses, sage, coltsfoot, mimosa, and caper bushes. By night, they settled on rust-colored sands amidst dwarf acacia and slept under starry skies.

But then the natural habits of the flock changed mysteriously. No longer did they lie peacefully at dusk and pass the night in quiet. Instead, they scampered and bleated, and leapt about nervously, with no apparent need for rest. Day after day and night after night, they romped inexhaustibly to and fro. And so, eventually, the herdsman reported to the imam that something was not right. The goats, he said, are too animated.

The head of the mosque came to where the indefatigable goats raced and played. "What do you think is the cause of their condition?" he inquired of the goatherd. "I do not know, holy sir, but I suspect the worst, that perhaps a *djinn* has cast a spell upon them, and that thus enchanted, they will dance upon the earth until they collapse and die from weariness!"

The imam had seen many things in his long years and favored

practical explanations rather than supernatural causes. "This condition is not likely the workings of a *djinn*," he replied. But he was curious that the goats had barely slept for seven days.

"Tell me," the imam spoke to the goatherd. "Have you noticed these animals eating anything out of the ordinary?" The herdsman tugged at his beard with distress and rubbed his pate, vexed over the question. He did not know the answer.

Since no solutions to the curious condition of the goats were readily forthcoming, the imam determined to watch the herd closely, observing everything the animals ate. "As a result of our careful observation, the truth shall be revealed." And so for a night and a day, the imam and his assistant and the agitated goatherd paid close attention to the goats, where they roamed and what they ate.

Eventually, the goatherd called out with excitement. "I believe I may have found the offending food!" In his hand, he held a spray of a shrub that neither of them could identify. Fragrant white blossoms projected from clusters of shiny green leaves, and the plant possessed small oval berries with hard kernels.

The imam took the spray and turned it over and over. In all his days, even as a learned man with knowledge of flora, he had never seen such a plant. "Are you certain the goats have eaten this?" he inquired.

The goatherd pointed to damaged branches and places where the teeth of the animals had chewed. "There can be no doubt about it, Oh great sir." The head of the mosque poked at the plant, sniffed at it, and bit off a small piece of a leaf, chewing it thoughtfully. What a strange thing. Oh mystery of mysteries!

The imam and his assistant and the goatherd collected a full armload of the newly discovered shrub, laden with its pretty flowers and strange berries. For the imam was not only learned in the teachings of the great prophet Mohammed, but he was also a keen-minded man of the sciences. Back at the mosque, he would study the plant.

Perhaps, he mused, the same invigorating effect which possessed the goats could also be felt by man.

In his chambers at Shehodet Mosque, the imam carefully inspected each part of the shrub, noting the skin of the branches, the color and shape of the leaves, the form and fragrance of its blossoms, and the peculiar berries, whose flesh contained a hard kernel.

In vessels of water, he methodically made various cold potations, one of the whole shrub, one of just the leaves, and one of just the berries, which he crushed with a pestle. Of each of these, he sipped one at a time, waiting to notice any effect. Nothing of any note occurred.

The imam also prized out the berry kernels, toasted them in a dish over a fire, and crushed them well with a pestle. Into a small pot of boiling water, he threw a generous handful of the powder. The water blackened and yielded pleasant, nutty vapors. After consuming a cupful of the hot infusion of the toasted berry kernels, the imam felt uncommonly invigorated.

"Mighty Allah!" he exclaimed to himself. How could a simple berry kernel be imbued with such power? The imam wondered with exceeding wonder, and his mind sprang alive, as a falcon takes to flight. Ideas and thoughts arose in great profusion. The imam felt his wit quicken, as though all his senses were keener. "Mighty Allah!" he exclaimed once more, just for good measure.

"No one can understand the truth until he drinks of coffee's frothy goodness."

~Sheik Abd-al-Kadir

Indeed, was this strange new plant not a gift from almighty Allah, may his name be praised? Never in his years had he come upon such a plant. Inspired by his discovery, the imam consulted the most learned of herbalists. But none had ever seen or heard of this strange tree.

After much rumination and consultation, the imam plucked from his memory something he had learned about Ethiopians who had migrated to Yemen centuries before. They came from the territory of Kaffa, and among the fruits and vegetables they brought with them was the kaffa tree. The plant was not wild, but domesticated in earlier times in another land.

Of all duties of faith in a mosque, none is as wearying a struggle as Tahajjud, the call to prayer in the dead of night. Sometimes the urge to remain asleep is so overpowering, it pulls one down into a weighted, mumbling stupor. Many is the faithful devotee who has fallen down and passed out during the unnatural privation of night prayers. Even if you can stay awake, your legs feel like wood, your arms like lead, your head stuffed with sackcloth. Anything that might improve wakefulness and ease the burden of fatigue would be a blessing.

With exactly this end in mind, the imam made a strong decoction of the crushed, roasted kaffa tree berry kernels. To awaken each devotee for night prayers, he offered a cupful of the steaming brew, which was black in color, bitter in flavor, and pleasing to the nose.

Each person accepted the cup and drank as instructed. Instead of dragging themselves about wearily, the pious shed all sense of fatigue, attending to prayer awake, alert, and in cheerful spirit. The faithful named the drink *k'hawah*, meaning stimulating and invigorating. From that time, coffee was served prior to Tahajjud to allay fatigue and enliven the minds of the pious.

The legend of coffee's discovery by a Yemeni Sheikh has in it not only the qualities of a good mystery, but something much more: divine inspiration. The providential discovery of coffee led to the relief of prayerful fatigue among the company of the faithful, the ardent devotees of Allah.

In time, coffee became pervasive throughout Islam, hailed as a divine agent that furthered mental alertness and promoted sobriety. Islam's strong opposition against the consumption of wine was greatly aided by the appearance on the scene of coffee. Here was a drink that worked magically upon the body and mind, in ways that furthered work and faith, instead of hindering them.

Coffee, the friend of the holy, would be carried like a standard across all of Allah's vast kingdom.

"In Damascus, Aleppo, and in the residence of Cairo, it has gone round with a great Hallo! The coffee bean, the scent of ambrosia! Then it entered the seraglio and the air of the Bosphorus, seducing Doctors, Cadis, and the Koran to sects and martyrdom! – And now it has triumphed! It supplanted in this happy hour, in the Moslem empire, wine which until then was consumed!"

- Turkish Poet Belighi

Chapter 4
The Great Coffee Awakening

During the years 1573 to 1578, the German physician, botanist, and explorer Leonhard Rauwolf traveled throughout Turkey, Syria, and Persia. Along the way, he documented the use of various plants and collected numerous specimens. Rauwolf wrote an account of his travels, *Reis in die Morganlander*, in which he was the first Westerner to describe coffee. The beverage made him feel "curiously animated."

In the course of his explorations, Rauwolf discovered that coffee was widely used among the general population, known at the time both as *chaube* and *bunnu*. Of this, he wrote, "Among other things, they possess a beverage which they value highly, called *chaube*. It is as black as ink and very useful in various diseases, especially those of the stomach. They usually take it in the morning in public without fear of being seen. They drink it from small earthen or porcelain cups, as hot as they can bear it. They frequently lift these vessels to their lips and take small sips, and then pass them round in the order in which they are sitting. They prepare a beverage from water and a fruit which the natives call *bunnu*. This somewhat resembles the laurel berry in size and color. This beverage is very much in use, and for this reason, a large number of merchants may be seen in the bazaars selling the fruits or the beverage."

Constantinople Coffee House

Rauwolf's account of coffee stirred interest among Europeans, who looked to the Orient for exotic goods, including silks and spices, from pungent black pepper to sweet cinnamon. Coffee was already widely consumed and traded when Rauwolf hit Anatolia or Asia Minor, with a known history that began around 700 years prior to the doctor's explorations. Almost certainly first consumed in Ethiopia, coffee was also enjoyed in Persia in 875, according to nineteenth-century plant researcher Ernst Von Bibra.

From what can be pieced together concerning coffee's uses through time, prior to the year 1000, members of the Ethiopian Galla tribe ground up coffee beans and mixed them with animal fat. This mixture they consumed as an energy food, very much the same way that native North Americans combined dried meats, nuts, berries, and tallow into a high-energy food known as pemmican.

"Coffee and love taste best when hot."

— African Proverb

Sometime around 1100, Arab traders brought coffee back to their homeland and cultivated the plant for the first time on plantations. Some historians maintain that the first plantations of coffee were made in Yemen, along the coast of the Red Sea. The Arabs found a more pleasant and palatable way to prepare coffee by boiling the beans. This resulted in a drink they call "*K'hawah* " (stimulating, energizing). By the late 13th century, Arabs roasted and ground coffee before brewing it, and coffee was consumed in a form similar to that of today.

As a hot beverage, coffee was well-positioned for its rise to world prominence. The reverie that a cup of hot coffee induces, of clarity, quickened wit, a refreshed spirit, and an invigorated body, would captivate humanity like no other substance on earth.

Among all plants, all foods, all drugs, coffee would become king. To achieve such an exalted status, coffee had to work its way into the hearts and minds of millions, insinuate itself into devious schemes, leap from country to country and continent to continent, and rise to stratospheric esteem in the imaginations of humanity.

Coffee Plantation

By the time the 15th century neared its close, Muslims had introduced coffee to Persia, Egypt, Turkey, and North Africa. Coffee became a major trade item, carried on the backs of humpy herds of camels, and was highly prized. The world's first coffee shop, Kiva Han, opened in the Ottoman capital of Constantinople in 1475.

A coffee shop may seem utterly ordinary today, but at that time, it was a stunning new concept. Turkish men and women alike took to the new drink with fervor. Coffee became a regular item of the Turkish diet and a measure of marital stability. So highly valued was the brew that Turkish law allowed a woman to divorce her husband if he failed to provide her with daily coffee!

Coffee faced harsh opposition in 1511, when Emir Khair Bey Mimar, the new governor of Mecca, attempted to ban the beverage and its consumption. Angered that he was being lampooned by critics, the governor determined to find out about those who spoke against him. When he discovered that his detractors were all coffee drinkers, his mood toward the beverage soured. He assembled a group of scholars, military leaders, and other learned men to discuss the drink.

The governor pressed for support in his opinion against coffee, pushing the notion that the drink was an intoxicant that violated Koranic law. But the august assemblage, many of whom were likely coffee enthusiasts, was loath to condemn the beverage.

At the end of a great deal of wrangling, the group of scholars declared coffee "*mekruh*," or undesirable. But their position fell far short of condemnation.

The angry Khair Bey Mimar was not deterred in his campaign. Fuming over the harsh comments leveled by coffee-consuming critics, he ordered all coffee houses closed, taking the position that coffee drinking led to riots.

For a week, coffee drinkers were abused in the most horrible ways, publicly humiliated, flogged, and driven out of town. But Sultan

Selim of Cairo, himself an ardent coffee drinker, refused to let the governor's order stand. He reversed the ban and allowed coffee houses to reopen, and further declared coffee beneficial to health and pleasing to God.

The incident became pivotal in coffee's march through time and culture. News of Khair Bey's humiliation spread throughout the Mohammedan world, resulting in elevated status for the beverage and increased trade in the bean. In this incident, coffee survived its first scrape with opposition. But it would not be the last.

"Actually, this seems to be the basic need of the human heart in nearly every great crisis - a good hot cup of coffee."

~Alexander King

As coffee use boomed at the termination of the Silk Road in Aleppo, as well as in Damascus and Cairo, so wine and the stores in which it was sold were driven out of business in the holy name of the Prophet Mohammed.

In 1554, coffee houses opened on the Golden Horn along the mighty Bosphorus and became known as schools of the cultured. Coffee was called the "milk of chess-players and of thinkers." By 1630, over one thousand coffeehouses operated in Cairo alone. Coffee facilitated conversation, and coffeehouses were places where ideas were exchanged. Today, it is hard to imagine the utterly revolutionary effect coffee exerted upon society.

Coffee drinkers assembled to share coffee and to discuss life, religion, politics, love, art, poetry, the sciences, virtually anything at all. Coffee was a revelation. The drinking of coffee in public places stimulated more conversation among people than any other event in history. Coffee pried loose the conversational jaws of the east and set in motion a history-changing exchange of thought. Today, it is hard to estimate how radical this was. But in the 1500s, coffee was unlike anything ever known. It was an unstoppable force, lightning in a cup.

"During the sixteenth, seventeenth, and eighteenth centuries, the ladies of Aleppo and Constantinople frequented the public baths, which were referred to as the Bagnio or Hummann. Coffee was served there, as the women remained for some time in the Bagnio, where they enjoyed drinking coffee, chatting, and bathing. Dashing water upon one another was a common frolic, and the Fouta or wrapper was easily dropped by accident or drawn aside in sport, and, should the girl happen to be carrying a cup of coffee at the time, she often continued and served it without stooping to recover her Fouta. This is the explanation of the fact that the women were sometimes seen in the Bagnio, walking about in the nude state as they carried coffee."

– Ralph Holt Cheney

From the lands of Mohammed's faithful, coffee marched mightily onward to Christendom, carried across the borders of Europe by Venetian traders. Around 1600 in Italy, Pope Clement VIII was urged by his priest advisers to ban coffee as an infidel threat.

The pope reputedly tasted coffee to ascertain for himself the nature of the drink. So enamored was he of its delicious flavor that, much to the annoyance of his grim advisors, he chose to "baptize" coffee instead, proclaiming that "coffee is so delicious it would be a pity to let the infidels have exclusive use of it." Hah!

Thus, Islam's dark and holy potion flowed hot and steaming into the heart and soul of Christendom with a graceful papal blessing. Coffee, that wonder-working potion, was assured a good passage into the lives of Catholics throughout Europe.

A dark and mysterious brew from the Moslem east, revered as a divine agent of sober and clear thought, coffee also became revered in Europe among all Christians for the same purposes. Coffee claimed a powerful stronghold and divine status in two of the world's greatest religions.

The European mind would be pried open, stimulated, and seasoned by flowing cups of the dark brew. The crowbar of this great opening of the gates of mentation was coffee. From the coffee pot flowed ideas and conversation, a great human exchange served piping hot.

"As long as Mocha's happy, tree shall grow,

While berries crackle or while mills shall go,

While smoking streams from silver sprouts shall glide,

Or China's earth receive the sable tide,

While coffee shall to British nymphs be dear,

While fragrant streams the bended head shall cheer,

Or grateful bitters shall delight the taste,

So long her honours, name and praise shall last."

- Alexander Pope

Chapter 5

Titan Of Commerce

As coffee grew in popularity, intrigue percolated around its cultivation. The Arabs, protective of their precious *Coffea arabica*, refused to allow fertile seeds, coffee trees, or cuttings to leave their countries. Transportation of the plant out of the Moslem nations was strictly forbidden by law. But sometime in the 1600s, a Sufi from India named Baba Budan snuck seven fertile coffee seeds out of Arabia. He planted his seeds in the hills in Mysore, India, where they flourished. Today, the hill plantations in the same region are populated with coffee trees descended from Baba Budan's smuggled beans. Regarded as a saint, Baba Budan's shrine can be found in Karnataka, India. I had occasion many years ago to sip coffee from the Mysore hills, and found it delicious.

In 1650, a Lebanese Jew named Jacobs opened the first coffee house in England, at Oxford. Coffee quickly became popular among students and teachers who established the Oxford Coffee Club. A 1671 publication described the event this way:

"This year, Jacob, a Jew, opened a Coffee house at the Angel, in the Parish of ST. Peter in the East, Oxon, and there it was by some, who delighted in the Noveltie, drank." Jacobs subsequently opened a second coffee house, Jacob's, in London's Holborn.

Two years later, a Greek from Ragusa named Pascal Rosee' opened the first coffeehouse in London, Pasqua Rosee's Coffee House, at St. Michael's Alley in Cornhill. The coffee house advertised *"The vertue of the COFFEE drink, first publiquely made and sold in England."*

In 1652, a merchant named Edwards, who had brought coffee from the Levant and a Greek slave girl from Smyrna, opened a coffeehouse in London as well. From that point on, coffeehouses proliferated in the great city, germinating conversation and ideas. Coffee spread like wildfire throughout all of London and beyond.

Coffeehouses became meeting places for merchants, politicians, and thinkers of all stripes, who found inspiration for their ideas in cups of coffee and partners in conversation. Coffee-inspired ideas, transactions, commerce, schemes, and political parties. Pamphlets, leaflets and publications of various kinds were available in coffeehouses, and not all of them were favorable to the crown.

Thus, shortly before New Year's Day in 1676, England's attorney general William Jones ordered all coffeehouses closed, citing harm to his Majesty King Charles II and the realm. The resulting public outcry was so overwhelming that the royal had no other option but to back down. Coffeehouses reopened for good, and the free flow of caffeinated ideas and opinions changed the shape of England. Coffee, with triumphant cheers from the adoring masses, pressed onward.

> *"Coffee falls into the stomach, and there is general commotion. Ideas begin to move like the battalions of the Great Army of the Republic on the battlefield. Things remembered arrive at full gallop... The light cavalry of comparisons delivers charges, the artillery of logic hurries up with trains and ammunition, the shafts of wit start up like sharpshooters. Similes arise, the paper is covered with ink; for the struggle begins and is concluded with torrents of black water, just like a battle with powder."*

> ### *- Honore' de Balzac.*

On a chill and cloudy October day, I walked about five misty miles from London's South Kensington to the Embankment along the River Thames, to London Bridge Road and then to Lombard Street, simply to stare at a plaque on a wall. As pilgrimages go, this one was modest. Edward Lloyd's coffeehouse opened in 1688 on Tower Street in London.

Three years later, the shop re-opened on No. 16 Lombard Street, where it operated for almost a century. The coffee house functioned as the business address of many merchants, and was from the start integrally involved with the shipping trade.

The business at Lloyd's greatly exceeded the brewing of coffee. Rather, the coffee house stood as a valuable meeting place for high trade and was profitable throughout its entire history. Now all that remains for the coffee history sleuth is a blue plaque reading "Site of Lloyd's Coffee House 1691 – 1785." This operation became the British insurance giant, shipping company, bank and numerous other global enterprises under the banner of Lloyd's of London. In 2011, the 17th-century frontage of the famous coffee house was exhibited for a while at the British National Maritime Museum in Greenwich. It is owned by Lloyds of London.

Lloyd's sign

By 1700, over two thousand coffeehouses operated within the city of London. Like the great River Thames itself, coffee, hot and fragrant, flowed through the densely populated urban capital of the mighty British Empire with immense force, sweeping people up by the tens of thousands. Coffeehouses were known as "penny universities," for a penny was charged for a hot cup of coffee and a quickening of the wit.

The word "TIPS" was coined in an English coffee house: A sign reading "To Insure Prompt Service" (TIPS) was placed by a cup. Those who wanted prompt service and a good seat wisely put a coin in the cup.

"The powers of a man's mind are directly proportioned to the quantity of coffee he drinks."

— James Mackintosh

While Jacobs was opening the first coffeehouse in England, the Dutch, mindful that coffee would be a huge and lucrative crop, began experimenting with its cultivation, with coffee plants from Mokha brought to Holland. In 1658, the Dutch began the cultivation of coffee in the Indian Ocean island of Ceylon. Dutchman Willem van Outhoorn, Governor-General of the Dutch East Indies, was determined to set up plantations in Java and Sumatra. The industrious Dutch planted coffee successfully there and on the verdant islands of Bali, Timor and Celebes, establishing Indonesia as a major producer of coffee, which it remains to this day.

Italy's romance with coffee commenced in the 1570s when a community of Turkish merchants moved into the Rialto, the commercial and financial heart of Venice. They came not only with goods from the Ottoman world, but also with coffee, which they enjoyed among themselves, as was their custom. This was confirmed when the possessions of a merchant named Huseyin Celebi were inventoried by police following his murder in 1775. Among his goods was found a traditional Arabic coffee cup without a handle called a finjan.

Prospero Alpini, a Venetian physician and professor of botany at northern Italy's University of Padua, imported coffee in the 1630s for sale in apothecaries. Prospero wrote several botanical books, including his well-regarded 1601 publication *The Presages of Life and Death in Diseases. His book De Medicina Egyptorium is believed to be the first work mentioning coffee published in the West.* Prospero considered coffee a valuable plant medicine. Thus, for a time, coffee was sold for its medicinal virtues. Prospero is also credited with introducing bananas to Europe, a remarkably diverse and talented man.

Historians dispute the date of the opening of Italy's first coffee shop. They probably even argue about it over coffee. It may have been when a Jewish merchant opened a café in the port city of Livorno on the Ligurian Sea in 1632, though some Italian historians say that the first shop in that country opened in Venice sometime after 1647 in Saint Mark's Square.

The oldest continuously operating Italian coffee shop is Caffe' Florian, established in 1720, also located in the square, which is also known as the Piazza San Marco. The place was frequented by literary figures and luminaries of all sorts, including Byron, Casanova, Proust, Dickens and Goethe. The café was originally called *Alla Venezia Trionfante*, Venice the triumphant.

As with cafés in other cities, Caffe Florian became a center for knowledge and the free flow of ideas, another penny university. But it also incurred the ire of state authorities as a place where seditious ideas might foment, and was shut down for a time by state inquisitors, to later re-open simply as Florian.

Ripening coffee cherries

As coffee and its ensuing conversations became popular in Italian cities and throughout the nation, Italy's inventive and stylistic spirit also transformed the drink forever with the invention of espresso, steam-expressed, finely ground dark coffee. The resulting beverage was more like a shot than a larger cup, strong and aromatic. The first espresso machine patent was awarded to inventor Angelo Moriondo in May of 1884, for "New steam machinery for the economic and instantaneous confection of coffee beverage, method *'A. Morindo.'*"

In 1901, Milanese mechanic and inventor Luigi Bezzera patented his *Bezzera L. Caffe' Espresso* machine with significant improvements and modifications from Moriondo's original model. Bezzera exhibited his invention at the 1906 World's Fair in Milan. The patent for Bezzera's invention was eventually sold to Desiderio Pavoni, who manufactured the espresso machines in Milan one at a time. Not only did Italians reinvent coffee by making a drink quickly via steam expression, they also took the lead in espresso machine development with brands like Cimbali, Bialetti, La Faema, Rancilio, Gaggia and many more.

Basically, they did what they would eventually do with sports cars and motorcycles and all manner of appliances, turning out sophisticated, elegant machines with style. The Italian espresso machines were also highly productive, making as many as several hundred small cups of very good coffee quickly. To this day, Italy remains an espresso culture, driven by gleaming invention and a lot of steam under pressure.

"Linked to the emergence of the public sphere and, by extension, modern democratic values, Western coffeehouses are effectively the descendants of the dynamic ... Arabic coffeehouse culture."

- **Neha Vermani**

Coffee inevitably spread to France, where the first coffeehouse in Paris was opened in 1689 by an Italian named Francois Procope. His Café de Procope was a major success and became a popular literary hangout and meeting place. By 1700, over 250 coffee houses operated in the city.

French innovation changed coffee drinking forever when they first made a different kind of infusion of the beverage. Up until that point, coffee was roasted, ground and boiled, and the resulting beverage was awash in grounds. By the ingenious French infusion method, ground coffee was placed in a cloth filter, over which boiling water was poured. This resulted in a cleaner, more refined and pleasant drink. The French also boiled milk and added it to coffee, making *café au lait* a popular breakfast beverage. Like the coffeehouses in other nations, those in France became centers for the free flow of coffee and ideas.

"Great is the vogue of coffee in Paris. In the houses where it is supplied, the proprietors know how to prepare it in such a way that it gives wit to those who drink it. At any rate, when they depart, all of them believe themselves to be at least four times as brainy as when they entered the doors."

- ***Baron de Montesquieu***

In Germany, coffee took off in 1721 with the opening of the first coffeehouse in Berlin. Within fifty years, coffeehouses operated in every major German city. Coffee became tremendously popular in Germany, though some stubborn physicians claimed that the drink caused sterility. In 1732, Johann Sebastian Bach composed his humorous ode to coffee, Coffee Cantata.

"Ah! How sweet coffee tastes! Lovelier than a thousand kisses, sweeter far than muscatel wine! I must have my coffee. There's no way to please me except with coffee."

- Coffee Cantata, Johann Sebastian Bach

In 1683, the Turkish Army surrounded Vienna. Franz Georg Kolschitzky, a Polish native and former interpreter for the Turks, slipped through the enemy lines to lead Polish relief forces to the city and to drive out the invading Turks, who were defeated in battle and fled Vienna. Among the many goods they left behind, the Turks abandoned five hundred sacks of "dry black fodder" that Kolschitzky recognized as coffee. For his heroism, Kolschitzky was offered any of the goods left behind by the Turks. He claimed the bounty of coffee as his personal reward and opened Vienna's first coffeehouse, House Under the Blue Bottle. In the habit of the Turks, Kolschitzky sweetened the coffee. He additionally filtered out the grounds and added milk. The resulting drink - sweet, fragrant, delicious and stimulating - caught on like wildfire.

Coffee sailed across the great Atlantic Ocean and made its way into the New World with aplomb. With the opening of the first coffeehouse in Boston in 1689, originally named the London Coffee House, coffee began its steady campaign to secure the ardent loyalty of North American colonists.

Tea was at that time the preferred caffeinated beverage in the new colonies, but that all changed in one eruptive burst with the famous Boston Tea Party of 1773, which was purportedly planned in

Boston's Green Dragon coffeehouse. Angry colonists resisting a tea tax imposed by Britain's King George threw bales of British East India Company tea into Boston harbor.

Shunning tea became a patriotic duty. And in that shining and decisive moment in history, coffee was taken up as the national beverage in a swelling tide of patriotic fervor. Coffeehouses flourished, the coffee trade boomed, and roasting operations sprang up like weeds to meet demand. From a single Boston coffeehouse, the United States would become the greatest coffee market in the world. By the early 1940s, the coffee-powered United States imported 70 percent of the world's coffee crop.

> *"Coffee - the favorite drink of the civilized world."*
>
> **– Thomas Jefferson**

Coffee intrigue continued in 1714, when Louis XIV of France was made a gift of a coffee tree by Mayor Brancas of Amsterdam. The tree was lovingly cared for in the royal greenhouses and jealously protected by its tenders. Enter French infantry captain Gabriel Mathieu De Clieu, Lieutenant of the King. Commissioned by the king to grow coffee on the tropical volcanic slopes of the island of Martinique, in 1723, De Clieu secured a seedling from the precious royal coffee tree.

With his botanical treasure under glass, De Clieu boarded a ship for Martinique. Braving attempted theft of the plant, pirates and rough weather, the determined Frenchman brought the seedling safely to the lush shores of Martinique. During the sea voyage, De Clieu apparently deprived himself of a large portion of his water ration to keep his precious cargo from drying. Twenty months after he stepped ashore with the prized seedling, a small crop of coffee cherries was harvested. Coffee fared well in Martinique. Fifty years later, an official survey recorded 19 million coffee trees on the island! Cultivation of the noble bean spread to Santo Domingo (Now Haiti), which became for a time a major coffee supplying nation. Mighty coffee continued to advance its position, establishing a domain in the Caribbean.

The gigantic Brazilian coffee industry also got off to an intriguing start in 1727, when a Brazilian official named Francisco de Melo Palheta was called upon to settle a border dispute between the French and the Dutch colonies in Guiana. Not only did he accomplish the task he was assigned, he also bedded the wife of French Guiana's governor as a bonus.

Though the French and Dutch guarded their coffee plantations to prevent cultivation from spreading, Palheta enlisted the governor's wife's willing aid in smuggling out some of the plant. When the good lady said goodbye to Palheta at the completion of his official mission, she presented him with a bouquet in which she hid coffee tree cuttings and fertile coffee seeds.

Palheta returned to Brazil and planted the coffee in the state of Pará. Through subterfuge, coffee made its way to a prime growing area and took root. But Brazil was different from all other places, and in time, the fertile South American nation Brazil would become the greatest coffee producer in all of history.

While coffee has played a giant role in the furtherance of conversation and commerce, it has also contributed to the power of the military. Coffee became an essential ration for Union soldiers during the grueling Civil War from 1861 to 1865. The noble bean figured heavily in World War II, when US defense workers and troops were supplied with as much coffee as they required. The Army alone requisitioned an astounding 140,000 bags of coffee per month, and the Marines boasted that they drank more coffee than any other branch of the service. Military provisioners roasted, ground and packed immense quantities of coffee.

On the war front, where conditions ranged from miserable to hellish, a hot cup of coffee often provided the only warmth, comfort and stimulation a soldier could find. Red Cross workers dispensed cups of coffee to battle-weary soldiers, and K rations included coffee as a matter of course.

A cup of coffee became so associated with US GIs that it became known as a "cup of Joe," referring to GI Joe, the military everyman. Patriotism, determination, superior arms and unbending will may have won World War II, but it was coffee, black coffee, that woke soldiers up, energized them, and gave them the extra margin of strength to press on in battle.

Coffee, the drink of patriotic Americans, was fought side by side with US soldiers in the war. And mighty coffee helped to bring home the win. To this day, even in the harshest battle areas in the world, coffee shops are established on US military bases to supply troops with the beverage.

"As long as there was coffee in the world, how bad could things be?"

- Cassandra Clare, *City of Ashes*

Roasted coffee

The history of coffee is rife with intrigue, politics, and the rise and fall of fortunes, and the story is far too great and vast to convey in full. But suffice it to say, coffee rules supreme among all crops. Today, coffee is grown in South America, Africa, Asia, Oceania, the Caribbean and Indonesia.

The coffee-producing nations include Angola, Bolivia, Brazil, Burundi, Cameroon, Central African Republic, Colombia, Congo, Costa Rica, Ecuador, El Salvador, Ethiopia, Gabon, Ghana, Grenada, Guatemala, Haiti, Honduras, India, Indonesia, Ivory Coast, Jamaica, Kenya, Madagascar, Martinique, Mexico, Nicaragua, Nigeria, Papua New Guinea, Rwanda, Tanzania, Togo, Uganda, US (Hawaii), Vanuatu, Venezuela, Vietnam and Yemen. Coffee brands such as Maxwell House and Nescafé' are known around the world. And corporations like Starbucks, Dunkin Donuts, Tim Horton's, Peet's, Caribou and Seattle's Best now fight for US café dominance, with Starbucks operating over 17,000 US locations in 2025.

Coffee has accomplished a mighty task. It has spread farther and wider than any plant; it has insinuated itself into the diets and kitchens of hundreds of millions of people, and it has spawned vast commerce. More than 400 billion cups of coffee are consumed each year. That's about 12,600 cups of coffee per second, 365 days a year. Wow. Bravo, coffee, bravo!

Chapter 6
Coffee, The Plant, The Triplets

Even with many of the most common items in our lives, we often don't inquire into their origin or history. Yet almost every day, many of us sit in coffee reverie as the smoky vapors of the world's most popular prepared beverage tease our olfactory bulbs and the bitter and complex flavors of the dark and mysterious brew dance over our tongues. What is this? From where does it originate? Who harvests the beans?

The broadly-consumed coffee bean derives from three species of the coffee tree (*Coffea arabica, canephora, liberica*), a pretty and highly productive work of nature. Coffee makes up the genus *Coffea* of the family *Rubiaceae*. Cinchona (*Cinchona pubescens*), the tree from which the anti-malarial compound quinine is derived, is also in this family, as is the popular if funky-smelling and grossly over-hyped health fruit noni (*Morinda citrifolia*). Arabian coffee is classified as *Coffea arabica*, robusta coffee as *Coffea canephora*, and Liberian coffee as *Coffea liberica*.

"I have measured out my life with coffee spoons."

- T. S. Eliot

Varying from 2 to 4 meters in height, the evergreen coffee tree features long, slender branches covered with bright, waxy, spear-shaped leaves. For those who don't think in metric amounts, 2 – 4 meters translates into 6.56 – 13.12 feet. The coffee tree bears both fragrant white flowers possessing a jasmine-like perfume and coffee cherries at the same time. Coffee beans are found inside the cherries.

The tree is also somewhat delicate, intolerant of sudden temperature changes, frost or heat exceeding 30°C. Again, for the non-metric, this means temperatures below 32°F or above 86°F. Coffee flourishes at higher altitudes, requires both sun and shade, needs plenty of water, and must be rooted in porous, well-drained soil.

In sub-tropical environments, arabica bean coffee grows between 1800 and 3600 feet in altitude. Sub-tropical areas (between 23.5 and 40 degrees of latitude in both hemispheres) have mean temperatures of 50°F or more for eight months out of the year. In the tropics and the "bean belt" (between the Tropic of Cancer at approximately 23° 26' 16" North and the Tropic of Capricorn at 23° 26' 16" South), coffee grows between 3600 – 6300 feet.

Tropical environments have mean temperatures all twelve months of the year above 18 °C (64 °F). When all the conditions in which it thrives are met, the coffee tree responds by producing a profusion of elliptic green cherries, which grow and ripen into bright red cherries half an inch long. These coffee cherries are picked at the peak of redness and then processed.

Ripe coffee

Coffee fruits, known commonly as cherries, are classified as drupes, featuring fleshy fruit surrounding a protected seed. Peaches, plums, mangoes, pistachios, almonds, nectarines and olives are also drupes.

When unripe, coffee cherries are a pale green. Upon ripening, they turn a shiny red. Inside the bright red skin of the coffee cherry is a gummy pulp surrounding a pair of facing beans bound together by a sweet, mucilaginous parchment. These are coffee beans.

When only one bean is found instead of two, it is referred to as a peaberry. Some people claim to be able to taste a difference between peaberry coffee and two-bean coffee. I'd love to put that claim to the test in a blind tasting, as it sounds like a fantastic exaggeration. Nonetheless, single or in pairs, coffee beans are green and waxy when picked out of their cherries.

Pop a green coffee bean into your mouth and chew it, and there is nothing at all to suggest that this waxy bean makes a good cup. Raw green coffee offers little appeal by way of flavor or aroma. But as we will learn later on, raw green coffee offers potent health benefits. As time goes on, we learn more and more. The discovery of green coffee's benefits is a major development in the history of this bean. What isn't especially good for the cup is very good indeed for health.

The Triplets of Coffee

Of the three species of coffee trees cultivated for commercial purposes, Arabica is the most highly prized. This is because Arabica of all varieties offers the most complex flavors and aromas, providing a superior drinking experience. Arabica coffee accounts for approximately 60% of coffee grown worldwide today.

One hectare (2.2 acres) of Arabica will produce between 1500 and 3000 kilos of beans. This is the original variety of coffee originating from Ethiopia, which spread throughout Islam, awakening the minds and bodies of the faithful. Arabica is the champagne of coffee.

All great-tasting coffees without exception, whether from Colombia, Papua New Guinea, Kenya or Jamaica, are arabica beans. The beans, and the way they are roasted, convey the various flavors and aromas for which various regional coffees are known and loved. Like fine wine grapes, arabica beans possess the subtle flavors of the soils and environments in which they are grown, conveying rich and heavy flavors in some areas, delicate and subtle flavors in others. Arabica coffee trees require five years of growth before they produce a good yield of ripe cherries, and the tree is less resistant to disease, especially the coffee-decimating leaf rust fungus *Hemileia vastatrix,* than the two other commercial varieties. If you love coffee, arabica is the brew to consume. A fine arabica bean coffee, roasted to perfection and prepared properly, is true satisfaction in a cup.

Like a brawnier, coarser cousin, the robusta species of coffee tree (*Coffea canephora*), which was discovered growing wild in the Belgian Congo, is much more hardy than the arabica tree, producing higher quantities of beans – between 2300 – 4000 kilos per hectare - with fully double the caffeine content. Think of robusta as truck-stop coffee. I have on many occasions driven for long hours in the dead of night on some journey, stopping along the way to tank up with gas and boost alertness with a cup of robusta. Robusta makes up around 40% of the coffee grown globally and goes into soluble coffee and canned grinds.

While arabica trees grow best at the elevations described above under specific climatic conditions, robusta trees can thrive in appreciably more variable environments. Robusta coffee is cultivated at much lower altitudes, between sea level and 3000 feet, in an area 10° North and South of the equator. Commercial robusta cultivation is primarily in Vietnam, West and Central Africa, and Southeast Asia. The trees do very well at lower elevations, and are suitable for planting in hot lowland plantations at temperatures that would wither arabica trees. Robusta trees produce a full crop yield in only two to three years after planting and are more resistant to disease.

Though robusta trees are hardy, robusta beans lack the flavor of arabica beans. Instead, robusta coffee is harsh and bitter. If arabica is the cognac of coffee, robusta is malt liquor. A 1912 New York Coffee

Exchange report criticized robusta as "a practically worthless bean," due to its flat, acrid flavor. Robusta beans have been known as simply carriers for caffeine, never noted for taste.

Instead, they are manufactured into instant coffee and the cheaper canned grinds. Now, in some places like Vietnam, growers are attempting to cultivate robusta for improved flavor. That road is long. Despite their lack of flavor, robusta bean coffees are very widely consumed. Highly caffeinated but lousy-tasting robusta beans supply fast food chains, diners, truck stops, donut shops and supermarkets with a concentrated and fast-acting stygian stimulant for a world on the go. Robusta coffee is a bulging bicep on the brawny musculature of world coffee commerce.

> *"Even bad coffee is better than no coffee at all."*
>
> **— David Lynch**

A rung further down on the flavor ladder is the Liberica coffee tree, native to West Africa. More hardy and more disease-resistant than arabica, liberica coffee trees grow higher than either arabica or robusta, and this variety is easily cultivated at sea level. Though the beans of this variety are comparatively large, Liberica yields are moderate. It is cultivated commercially in Malaysia and West Africa, and there only in relatively small quantities. Liberica beans are used as filler beans in low-quality coffee blends and account for less than 1% of global coffee production. If arabica is champagne and robusta is malt liquor, liberica is jug tokay. Nobody drinks Liberica coffee for taste.

Varietals

When I was a kid, there was coffee and decaf. My grandmother bought Eight O'Clock Coffee from the A&P supermarket and ground it in a big red machine at the end of the cash register line. A sign on the grinder read "Taste the difference of fresh ground Eight O'Clock Bean Coffee." My parents drank pre-ground Yuban from a vacuum-packed can and prepared it in a Universal Coffeematic Percolator in the kitchen.

On TV, the legendary Juan Valdez of Colombian coffee fame sat astride a donkey laden with sacks of beans amidst lush plantations. Supermarkets featured Maxwell House (which annually has published an edition of the Passover Haggadah starting in 1932 and ever since), Chase and Sanborn, Folgers and Hills Brothers brands. Times were simple.

Eight O Clock coffee grinder

The days of few coffee choices are gone, the way of rotary phones and transistor radios. Today, coffee has traveled the path of wine. Whatever flavors, roasts or origins you seek, you can find them in the highly diverse coffee market of today.

Now you can acquire varieties of coffee from every producing country and from differing regions within those countries. Name your favorite - Yemeni Mocha Matari, Sumatra Gayo Mountain, Jamaican Blue Mountain, Hawaiian Kona, Colombian El Supremo, Ethiopian Sidamo, Kenya AA and hundreds more - there are a plethora of varietal coffees for sale. There are even some very far out and outrageously expensive gourmet coffees (as much as $600 per pound) like Kopi Luwak, which is produced from coffee beans that have gone through the digestive systems of Asian palm civets and excreted.

Elephant dung coffee, also known as Black Ivory Coffee, undergoes the same digestive process but through the massive GI tracts of elephants, boasting flavor notes of cacao, Pu-Erh tea, tamarind, date, plum and tobacco. Purportedly, the digestive process catalyzes novel and exotic enzymatic changes in coffee flavor and aroma. Post excretion, both varieties of coffee are cleaned thoroughly prior to roasting.

Each coffee variety tastes of the soil and climate conditions of its growing region. Organically grown coffees, in addition to being safer due to the absence of toxic agricultural chemicals, impart even more flavor and aroma, still, due to good agricultural practices that build richer soil. Each variety of coffee has its perfect roast, from light to dark. It's the job of the roaster to artfully tease out the maximum flavor and aroma of each variety by roasting the beans for just the right amount of time, at just the right temperature.

The popularity of varietal coffees has transformed the coffee market, providing opportunity for small and boutique growers and roasters to get in on a market that used to be dominated entirely by large companies that blended all coffees together.

The beans of the coffee tree are what all of coffee commerce is about, for it is the simple coffee bean which bears the bracing stimulant caffeine, in a form which, when properly prepared, also yields satisfying flavor and pleasing aroma.

Throughout the tropics and sub-tropics globally, an estimated 125 million people's lives depend upon the coffee crop. Millions more work in coffee processing, roasting, manufacturing, shipping, wholesale, in retail stores and of course behind counters at cafés everywhere. Not only is coffee a global wakeup agent, but its trade feeds, shelters and houses millions. This bean has spawned a multinational industry that never sleeps. Twenty-four hours a day, somebody in the world is harvesting coffee, or roasting it, or shipping it, or making an espresso. The simple coffee bean is an Atlas of commerce, a mighty titan that has amassed a gigantic global workforce.

Chapter 7
The Precious Beans Of Kona (2000)

A warm breeze blew through open car windows as three of us cruised the Kona coast on the western side of the big island of Hawaii. The October sun shone warm, and the aroma of coffee roasting somewhere nearby caught my attention.

"Yeah, this whole area, for about twenty miles or so, is nothing but coffee," noted my friend Zachary Gibson, who rode shotgun as I drove. In the back seat Zack's wife Hanna remarked at the sight of thousands of beautiful coffee trees heavily laden with ripe red coffee cherries.

Producing on average around 3,950 pounds of ripe cherries per acre, the healthy, mature trees we saw represented a whole lot of coffee. "Look at all those there," Zack called out, pointing to a perfectly manicured plantation.

Kona Arabica coffee

We had dropped onto the twenty mile long Kona Coffee Belt at its northern end at Palani Junction, and were making our way south through the heart of coffee country, where for over 200 years generations of growers have toiled to make Kona beans distinguished and prized among the world's great coffees. We admired what we could see of the 3,000 acres of coffee trees planted in the region (now around 3500 acres), whose fortunes have risen and fallen like the great Pacific swells which crest and break on Hawaii's rugged coasts.

In the 1950's, 6,000 acres of coffee grew on those hills, during a vigorous recovery period after a bad market collapse which followed a previous coffee boom. In its rising and falling, Kona's coffee fortunes were similar to those of Brazil and other coffee-producing nations. Boom and bust, planting and tearing out trees, have been cyclical aspects of coffee since it ever became a commercial crop. As coffee prices rise, growers plant more trees. As prices fall, trees are ripped out of the ground, and plantations go belly up.

Kona coffee plantation

Hawaii's affair with coffee began simply in 1825, when the Governor of Hawaii Chief Boki introduced coffee plants he had obtained in Rio de Janeiro, Brazil. In 1828 the Reverend Samuel Ruggles, a missionary, introduced the first coffee trees to Kona, near Kealakekua.

While the first Hawaiian commercial plantings of coffee were made on the island of Kauai, coffee failed there and was replaced by sugar cane. But on the big island of Hawaii, the districts of Kona on the island's west coast and Hamakua on the east coast provided good conditions for the delicate trees. The Kona Coffee Belt especially proved ideal for the growing needs of coffee trees.

Situated between the enormous Mauna Kea volcano to the north and Mauna Loa volcano to the south, the Kona Coffee Belt lay protected from damaging winds. Additionally, Kona benefits from bright, sunny mornings and shady afternoon clouds. These atmospheric conditions, plus the volcanic soil, good elevation and ample rainfall make Kona an excellent location for coffee.

The multitudinous forces of nature have melded together in harmonious perfection to make for coffee an ideal home on the lush green slopes of Kona. Today the higher grades of Kona coffee are sought after by aficionados worldwide who enjoy the rich flavor and aroma of that area's magnificent coffee.

Kona's coffee history is a story of boom and bust cycles. In the 1890's world coffee prices increased, and this inspired investors to plant coffee plantations in Kona. Chinese, Portuguese and Japanese laborers planted trees of the Typica variety of *arabica* coffee, pruned them, picked the ripe cherries at harvest, and put their backs into Kona's first lucrative coffee boom.

In Kona coffee grew well between 700 and 2,000 feet, but farmers had problems with coffee crop losses due to white scale blight. In 1893 the Ladybird beetle was introduced from Australia, and this proved successful in controlling the white scale disease. Coffee plantations thrived. While the introduction of a foreign species often turns into a disaster, in the case of the Ladybird beetle, Kona coffee was saved.

By 1900, a glut of beans on the world market led to Kona's first coffee bust as prices crashed. With fortunes lost, investors left the area with their pockets turned out and Chinese and Portuguese laborers moved away from the shady coffee orchards of Kona to perform harsh labor in hot, sunny lowland cane fields. There they toiled with machetes in the broiling sun for pitiable wages. What coffee remained in Kona was primarily cultivated by Japanese tenant farmers on small family plots.

Hawaiian coffee grower

By 1910, four out of five coffee farmers in Kona were Japanese. Husbands, wives and children worked the coffee, delivering ripe cherries to either one of the two dominant processing mills, Captain Cook Coffee Company or American Factors, which was originally known as H. Hackfeld and Co. The two processors controlled approximately 70 percent of the total coffee acreage of Kona. The coffee industry prospered again and remained strong up through and beyond World War I. The war was terrible for humanity but good for coffee.

Kona coffee prices rose steadily until 1928, and Japanese farmers prospered. But the stock market crash of 1929 caused coffee prices to crash as well to an all-time low. Between 1930 and 1940, the number of Japanese-owned Kona coffee farms dropped from 1070 to 600.

Despite this drop, by 1934 nine coffee mills in Kona were Japanese owned and operated. Transportation of coffee was performed by donkeys, which were known as "nightingales," due to their loud braying. Laden with 100 pound sacks of ripe coffee cherries, the donkeys had the sure-footedness and strength required to haul loads up and down steep hills and to the coffee mills.

Between 1941 and 1945, the Kona coffee industry was turned on its ear by World War II, which saw many Japanese coffee growers from Kona volunteering for military service. After the devastations and casualties of the war, Kona's coffee fortunes rose again with increases in world coffee prices. By 1959, twelve pulping mills operated in Kona and coffee prices began a giddy slide downward toward financial crisis, spelling yet another bust period.

The Kona coffee market might have stayed down, if not for the sophisticated needs and palates of an emerging social group of gourmet coffee drinkers in the late 1970's and 1980's. The new demand for expensive, regional gourmet coffee stimulated growth and production, and sent Kona coffee prices upward.

Kona Coffee Cherries

Kona's coffee fortunes were threatened during this time of growth by an insidious force, dilution. Kona "blends" flooded the coffee market, containing as little as 10% real Kona coffee. These blends, which can still be found today, typically a mix of a little Kona coffee and a lot of cheap, harsh beans, diminished the fine Kona name. These coffees should rightly be labeled "90% inferior blends."

Only a strong 100% Kona Coffee campaign has pulled Kona beans back up to the elevated position they so richly deserve. The only real Kona coffee is 100% Kona coffee. All diluted blends which use the Kona name are knock-offs which cannot, and do not, deliver. For while Kona "blends" often taste mediocre, properly roasted 100% Kona coffee is heaven in a cup.

Sun drying Kona coffee

As Zachary, Hanna and I motored along, we were in search of a small plantation, and a perfect cup to boot. For this, we sought out coffee grower Russell Archibald in Honaunau. We cruised up a steep drive lined on both sides by ten foot high coffee trees hanging heavily with green and red cherries, with some branches so laden they touched the ground. A medium-sized dog ran toward the car and barked at us ferociously. When we failed to respond in any way, the dog turned, wagged its tail and trotted back to the house. Obviously an ambivalent watchdog, he had performed his duty, and was thoroughly done with the matter.

On the porch Russell Archibald and his wife Mickey waved at us. He wore a sixties-style bandana from which a braid of long gray hair ran down his back, and she sported a colorful flowy dress from another era. Their home, made of weathered wood and surrounded by a riot of flowers in bloom, conveyed a welcoming feel. They invited us to their kitchen. There amidst a profusion of potted plants, we sat down around a worn wooden table. "Would you folks like some coffee?" Russell inquired.

In an old grinder, Russell finely whizzed dark-roasted arabica beans from his small plantation and placed them in a cloth strainer which he hung over a dented coffee pot. He boiled water in an old metal kettle on a gas stove, and poured the boiling water onto the coffee. Fragrant vapors steamed into the air, and I leaned in to sniff. The coffee when served was dark and strong, with a nutty cocoa aroma. Tremendous. An exquisite cup. Russell smiled warmly, and we all smiled, and sat drinking lovely coffee in big cups on a warm, sunny morning on the Kona coast, while birds sang and the scents of exotic blossoms wafted in the air.

Russell Archibald turned to me "Have you ever seen coffee harvested?" I hadn't, I said. He invited me to follow, and stepped out of his kitchen and into the back yard where he selected a woven basket from a pile of several, secured it to his waist with a belt, and headed toward coffee trees laden with red cherries. Russell explained that he grew his coffee by organic methods, without insecticides or fungicides. The trees looked healthy. Running his hands along the slender branches, he carefully plucked ripe cherries with a quick, practiced motion and laid them carefully in the basket. "This basket will hold about twenty pounds of coffee. I used to farm vegetables," Russell commented "but then I figured I couldn't make any money at it. I can make a little with coffee." Very quickly he collected at least a pound of coffee. In the lower elevation of the two mile wide Kona coffee belt in Honaunau where Russell grows his two acres of trees, coffee cherries usually ripen and are harvested between August and February. In the cooler and wetter higher elevations of the belt, coffee harvesting may go on all year long. A few hundred feet in elevation can make a big difference for a coffee farm.

Russell Archibald harvests coffee

Coffee is not an overly lucrative crop, and I muse over the economics of being a grower. Approximately 6 pounds of ripe cherries result in one pound of green beans, which when roasted will lose twenty percent of their weight. Thus 7.5 pounds of cherries are required to produce 1 pound of roasted coffee. In the 2022 season growers in Kona received 2.26 dollars per pound of cherries from processors. According to the State Of Hawaii Department of Agriculture, in the 2022 season an acre of mature coffee trees yielded an average 3,950 pounds of cherries, worth $8927. At those yields, a grower needs to harvest eleven acres of coffee to gross $100,000. That's a lot of physical labor in the heat. Plus, nobody picks that much coffee alone.

Kona Coffea arabica

An experienced picker can gather between 200 to 400 pounds of coffee cherries per day. Considering that coffee must be picked at peak ripeness and cannot be left to over-ripen, numerous pickers must work a farm. This provides hourly wage jobs for pickers, and reduces profits for growers. Coffee fruit on coffee trees does not ripen all at once.

In Kona, between four to eight passes through a coffee plantation each harvest season are required to pick ripe cherries. And yet hundreds of individuals like Russell Archibald, who has grown a small amount of high quality Kona coffee for many years, remain devoted to the crop. Maybe a big part of that is due to the sheer beauty of the plantation, lush, green, a profusion of fragrant blossoms, a riot of trees whose cherries yield a precious prize.

"There are times of great beauty on a coffee farm. When the plantation flowered in the beginning of the rains, it was a radiant sight, like a cloud of chalk, in the mist and the drizzling rain..."

- Isak Dinesen Out of Africa

56

Down the road from Russell and Mickey Archibald's place, at Greenwell Farms in Kealakekua the Greenwell family has produced high quality Kona coffee for over one hundred years. Operating 40 acres of their own coffee trees and buying from hundreds of other growers in the area, Greenwell processes Kona coffee from beginning to end, and sells it under their own label. This results in far greater profits than selling coffee cherries wholesale.

Before going through their processing facilities, Zachary, Hanna and I sampled several Greenwell coffees from pump-thermoses. I found the peaberry and stayed with it, the perfect flavor and roast for an afternoon pick-me-up.

Seedlings at Greenwell Coffee

Emerald Freitas, whose Portuguese grandmother farmed coffee for decades in Kona, showed us around the Greenwell processing facilities. Tens of tons of coffee beans dried on shed roofs, and a group of men were milling beans nearby.

A large nursery was filled with seedlings to replace old trees that no longer bore significant enough fruits. But what captured my attention most was the fragrance of roasting.

About this Emerald shared some of the specifics of the delicious Greenwell roasts. "We basically have three roasts, regular, city and dark. We roast all our beans at exactly 415øF. The regular roast goes for 16.5 minutes, the city roast goes for 18 minutes, and the dark roast goes for 19.5 minutes."

"On the nose?" I asked.

"On the nose."

Making The Grade

Even some Kona coffees cannot be labeled as such, as they fail to conform to certain quality standards. The five grades of coffee produced in the region are Extra fancy, Fancy, Hawaii No.1, Hawaii Select and Prime. There is also Hawaii No. 3, which contains a high amount of defective or sour beans. Kona coffees are graded according to screen size, cleanliness, color, moisture content, roasting quality, and their flavor and aroma when brewed. No. 3 grade is inferior coffee, and may not be labeled with the Kona coffee designation.

Peaberries, the small, single berries which account for less than 5% of the total Kona coffee yield, are graded separately. Peaberries are believed to be more flavorful by some coffee drinkers, according to the theory that a single bean within a coffee cherry has a different shape than two beans and therefor different roasting characteristics. Maybe. One thing is certain, peaberries typically command a high price among the gourmet coffee cognoscenti.

Ripening Kona coffee

Kona's legendary coffee deserves its fine reputation and high market price. On Hawaii's Kona coast the growing conditions for excellent coffee have all come together in perfect harmony. With careful tending of trees, harvesting cherries at peak ripeness and roasting just right, Kona's coffee results in a delightful cup.

Bad Ass Coffee Kona

Chapter 8
From Green Beans to Delicious

Once coffee is harvested, the cherries have about 24 hours to be processed before they start to soften. In the first of four steps, the pulping process, ripe coffee cherries are rotated in a drum and squashed. The pulp of the fruit is ejected, and the coffee beans, covered with a mucilaginous parchment, slip through grooves and are ejected out of the opposite side of the machine.

Next the slippery coating of the coffee bean must be removed, in a process called demucilaging. This is most often accomplished by fermenting the beans in a vat with bacteria that break down the coating until it easily dissolves in water. After fermentation, the beans are washed and the coating is gone. Next they are ready for drying.

Coffee beans are dried either in the sun, in mechanical rotary dryers, or on shallow drying trays subjected to hot air. They should not be heated over 150øF, or they lose aroma. The coffee beans, when dried, still retain a parchment skin around them. In the final stage of coffee processing, the beans are milled in hulling machines, removing the parchment. The resulting green coffee beans are ready for the process which transforms them into something fragrant, delicious, spoken of in holy terms.

After all the work required to strip coffee beans of their many layers, you'd think they would appear special somehow. In fact, milled coffee beans offer modest visual appeal. Dull green and waxy, they are not at all what one conjures in the mind when thinking of a steaming, fragrant cup of coffee. To become dark, aromatic and delicious, coffee beans must be roasted. Great roasts are works of art. Roasting sets in motion hundreds of chemical changes in coffee beans. Sugars decompose, gases are released, and a plethora of natural compounds are modified.

Coffee's aromas can vary widely and may include scents of pepper, maple, malt, clove, black currant, coriander, cedar, tobacco, lemon, rose, apple, potato, honey, apricot, cucumber and more. The seemingly endless scents of coffee owe to location of cultivation, climate, weather, rainfall, ripeness at harvest, steps of processing and roasting. Coffee roasting is an alchemical process by which waxy green beans are transformed into gold.

Antique coffee roaster World Coffee Museum Buon Ma Thuot

"Coffee you dispel the worries of the great...you are the drink of the friends of God...You are the common man's gold, and like gold, you bring to every man the feeling of luxury and nobility. You flow through the body as freely as life's blood, refreshing all that you touch. Oh drink of God's glory, your purity brings to man only well-being and nobility."

-Sheikh Ansari Djerzeri Hanball Abd-al-Kadir

Not every coffee processor is as exacting or fastidious as Greenwell in Kona, and various roasters have their preferred temperatures and times. But one thing is undeniable, that the roast makes the coffee. You need great beans to yield a great coffee. But it is the roast that exalts the coffee bean, the roast which gives a waxy green bean its exotic aroma and heavenly flavor, the roast which is tasted in the cup.

Predictably, people prefer different roasts according to taste. Some coffee drinkers like their brew on the lighter side, just as some wine drinkers prefer whites. I always prefer a city roast of heavy-flavored Indonesian or African beans, for a dark, ponderous cup. And give me a deep rich red wine any day, a California cabernet or an Italian Barolo.

In the earlier centuries of coffee's march around the world, roasting was more often accomplished at home. In pie plates, in frying pans or in the oven, coffee beans were heated and stirred until they evenly achieved the right color. Now few people roast beans at home. Coffee is either roasted in giant processing facilities, or in smaller, more boutique roasting operations.

So how do roasts settle out in terms of flavor?

Light roast –For delicate or mild-flavored beans, light roast is preferred by those who want coffee with a more sparing flavor.

Medium roast – This results in a darker coffee, with more flavor. The typical roast enjoyed by most American coffee drinkers.

Full roast – A very dark bean, and a very dark cup of coffee, imparting bold aroma and flavor. Also called a city roast.

Very dark roast – Not a roast for most people's preferred cup of coffee, the very dark roast is reserved for espresso beans and imponderably heavy Turkish coffee. After you drink Turkish coffee, you read the sludgy grounds at the bottom of the cup. Omens and signs can be discerned in the thick black goo.

Chapter 9
The Wizard of Coffee (2000)

Right around the turn of the millennium I was researching cacao (cocoa) in northern Venezuela when a friend named K.C Miller told me about a man who supposedly made the perfect cup of coffee. Not just excellent mind you, but perfect.

Apparently if you wished to experience that perfect cup of coffee, it was necessary to travel to Caracas. It seemed a small effort, considering the payoff. Curiosity piqued, my good friend Craig Weatherby and I headed to Caracas, the capitol of Venezuela. There in the Altamira section of that bustling equatorial city, French Canadian Jean Paul Coupal ran Arabica Café and Café Coupa roasters. To say that Jean Paul was a fanatic doesn't begin to describe the level of zeal and vigor he brought to coffee.

Coupal combined unbridled fanaticism with a quick and brilliant mind, an apparently insatiable appetite for knowledge, an uncompromising willingness to go to any extreme, an obsessive sense of absolute perfection, and an infectiously delightful manner of speech and behavior, all fused together in his passion for coffee. It took but one brief hour in his all-consuming company to recognize that Jean Paul Coupal was a Merlin of the coffee art.

"I have figured that there are a minimum of 120 steps in the coffee process in which quality can be maintained or degraded," Coupal explained, the fever of his coffee fanatic aura heating the side of me near him.

"I've also figured how to control every single one of them. It's an extraordinary task, but it's the only way to guarantee absolutely perfect coffee, from cultivation to roasting and preparation." I was only partly listening. Most of me was otherwise engaged in the soaring, divine experience of a cup of his espresso.

A layer of foamy crema in my cup, resulting from perfect steaming, looked like milk. But in fact it was all coffee, the sign of an exquisite cup, one whose bitterness is muted and delightful, a cup whose flavors and aromas dance all over the tongue and ping brilliant aromas against the olfactory bulb, a swooning cup, the Mozart of cups, a cup that can pick you up and dance you down the street and into the hills. I told myself that I must pay attention; the master was speaking.

I often marvel at the intricacies of other people's paths. When Jean Paul Coupal first drank Venezuelan coffee, it so impressed him that he endeavored to discover the various fincas in that country. But searching through trade archives in Venezuela yielded scant information.

The only way he could manage the task was to travel to Europe, and chase down the former buyers of coffee from Venezuela's Blohm & Abbott, who used to export coffee to Europe. Going through old files from coffee purchasers, Coupal found bills of lading which identified Venezuelan growers who used to supply Blohm & Abbott. By working backwards toward Venezuela in this manner, Jean Paul established contact with those growers who were still in business, and his determined march toward coffee perfection began.

"Thanks to government intervention in the coffee industry, Venezuelan coffee quality has plummeted over the last thirty years," Coupal explained.

"The government has pushed a low grade, robusta/arabica blend (arabusta) that's very high yield. And this has degraded Venezuelan coffee. It's such a shame, because Venezuela is home to some extraordinary bourbon criollo single varieties of coffee. These are the only coffees I'll use. I'll put these coffees up against beans from anywhere."

Jean Paul Coupal with Probat roaster

Jean Paul's Arabica Café' opened in 1991, a shrine to the highest coffee art. Inside, a gleaming Probat roaster dominated a quarter of the floor space. Near the front window, a UNIC espresso machine sat like a buddha in a stupa. "This machine is the Rolls Royce of coffee makers," Jean Paul told us. "It's made in Nice, France by a bunch of Italians, and nobody makes a machine that even comes close. It's the only machine I would use here."

Described by France's Liberation Magazine as "the man who wants to be coffee king of Venezuela," Jean Paul established Arabica Café as a bastion of coffee excellence, and the front line against coffee mediocrity. Antique Yemeni brass coffee pots lined shelves. Coffee artwork from around the world adorned the walls. Turkish made glass apothecary jars with brass tops displayed single estate, single variety coffees.

"Coffee is like wine," said Jean Paul. "You have a cabernet grape grown in a certain valley and made into wine by a certain winery, and it has particular characteristics. The same is true with coffee. Beans from one plantation will differ from beans from another. If you control all the quality steps and roast each bean to best bring out its own unique flavors and aromas, you get exquisite coffee." I could not argue any of it. Lifting the brass tops of one jar after another, I hovered above each, taking in the aromas of coffees from fincas named La Estancia, La Hacienda, La Orchieda.

Jean Paul Coupal started a modest but potent coffee revolution in Venezuela. Beginning with only two fincas, he eventually helped to reinvigorate and obtain coffee from eighteen fincas. His Arabica Café was a mecca for the coffee cognoscenti, who literally flocked from all over the world to marvel at what he accomplished and to drink his perfect coffee. Howard Schultz of Starbucks went there. So did legendary Boston chef Julia Child. A long list of coffee cognoscenti and gourmet chefs from the four corners of the earth went there. They were all humbled and uplifted.

Venezuelan coffee at Arabica Café'

Jean Paul Coupal was written up in dozens of magazine articles. People sent him their credit card numbers, asking him to ship them coffee, never inquiring about the price. The list of celebrity chefs, gourmands, food writers, entertainers and government officials who made the pilgrimage to Arabica Café would comprise an impressive volume of Who's Who.

Jean Paul's successful roasting business Café Coupa served offices, hotels, and restaurants. He placed espresso machines at gas stops all over the Caracas area and supplied them with superior beans. You could pull into a BP station, fill your tank and drive away with a banging cup of excellent espresso. His volume of production was significant enough that he revived both traditional basket weaving on coffee plantations, and a sisal bag factory.

In the case of baskets, Coupal insisted that all coffee picked for his enterprise must be put into woven natural fiber baskets, not plastic pails. This kept alive a dying art, providing a livelihood for numerous women artisans.

In the case of the sisal bags, Coupal was unwilling to use available woven bags whose fibers were lubricated with petroleum oils, which is the norm. Instead, he revived Fibro Textil in Barquisimeto, Venezuela, who lubricated their fibers only with vegetable oils. "You have to control everything," he declared. "It all makes a difference."

Sitting in front of Arabica Café on a warm, moderately humid, equatorial morning, Craig and I each sipped a tall café negro, with perfect crema. Puffy white clouds chugged across a blue sky. A slight breeze stirred the leaves of trees nearby.

A pair of vultures, as elegant as any birds in the air, rode a thermal over a high building without flapping a wing, and disappeared. I sipped slowly, letting the cup linger at my lips, allowing the aroma to waft upward into my nose. The exquisite grace of the moment overtook me, and I was suffused with reverie.

Craig Weatherby drinks Jean Paul Coupal's coffee

Jean Paul Coupal has since died but his titanic legend lives on. His daughter Nancy Coupal runs three Coupa Cafés in Palo Alto California. Was Coupal's coffee a perfect cup? Yes. Was the hype about Jean Paul Coupal real? Without doubt. I can say unequivocally that I have drunk the best cup of coffee ever made, in Caracas Venezuela. Was it worth the trip? Oh yes.

Chapter 10
How To Drink Coffee

Many is the time I have stood in a line in a café while patron after patron orders a large caramel whip macchiato, or a frozen coffee frappe' with whipped cream. This is not coffee. These are fluid desserts, or candies, and have absolutely nothing to do with the flavor and aroma of a good cup of coffee or its health benefits.

The ideal cup of coffee is drip grind, drunk black and unsweetened. If black coffee is not your cup of Joe, then a little milk is fine. A latte' is a cup of hot milk with a small amount of espresso. Forget it. A cappuccino, containing espresso and some steamed milk, is okay as a treat.

Espresso, which is finely ground coffee expressed with steam is fine, straight up. Forget cream, sugar, whipped cream, hazelnut syrup or any of the other fatty or sugary additives people use to turn perfectly healthy coffee into diabetes-causing high calorie delivery systems.

As for the myriad of chemical sweeteners out there, forget them entirely. They are unhealthy additives that have no place at all in the human diet. A cup of coffee, as described in this book, is either black coffee straight up, or coffee with a modest amount of milk.

Chapter 11
A Syrian Cup 2001

At 9:00 a.m. Hassan the driver arrives at the Summerland Hotel in Beirut to take me and my traveling partner Travis Hammond on the 110 kilometer trip across the Beqaa Valley to Damascus Syria. Upon entering the lobby of the hotel Hassan greets us with a somewhat sheepish look on his face.

"The radiator is broken," he explains with an apologetic shrug, referring to the car that is our reserved transportation. "Maybe we go around 2:00? Can we wait?" It seems unwise to waste much of the day hoping that the radiator will be fixed, knowing that such time estimates are often meant to please and cannot be trusted. I immediately go to the front desk and speak with the concierge about another car.

The Summerland is a lovely place in a beautiful spot, built around a large swimming pool and perched on the southeastern shore of the Mediterranean Sea. But we have business in Damascus and have no good reason to hang around.

Another most excellent reason to get on the road is that the coffee at the otherwise lovely Summerland Hotel is Nescafe', which seems inconceivable to me. How is it that here in the Middle East, a land famously known for its great steaming cups of fabulous arabica bean coffee, are we in a fine hotel where the fare offered is Nescafe', made from robusta beans? Last night while wandering Beirut's trendy Achrafieh district we came upon a vintage Volkswagen van with an old copper-domed Faema espresso machine set up in the open back, the night scene lit by a kerosene lamp and two men sitting on folding aluminum chairs playing backgammon. The aroma was lovely. Now that's coffee.

In less than half an hour an alternate driver named Mahmoud shows up at the hotel in a white Chevy Caprice, maybe one of the very first to come off the Janesville, Wisconsin assembly line in 1965.

The well-worn sedan sports a faded and flecked paint job, scrapes, dings and dents and almost bald tires. The front bumper is secured on one side by a bent coat hanger. It is a car nobody will likely attempt to steal.

As we will discover the Caprice rides on ancient shock absorbers, poor brakes and no seat belts for our dash to Damascus. I have taken the time and care to obtain a visa to enter Syria, so I will be able to breeze through customs. By contrast Travis has not done so and this will certainly cause a delay in getting into that country. Some things you can tell from a long way off.

We rage through smoggy Beirut, past bombed and shot buildings pocked with bullet holes from the 16 – year Lebanese civil war from 1975 to 1990, through snarled traffic and up into the cool Lebanese Mountains.On the eastern slope we barrel down into the 120 km long and 16 km wide Beqaa Valley, part of the Great Rift Valley stretching from Syria to the Red Sea. The verdant Beqaa accounts for more than forty percent of Lebanon's arable land, featuring crops of maize, wheat, cotton, vegetables, fruit orchards and vineyards. The valley is also famous for its opium poppies and for the pinkish-blond hashish made from its fragrant landrace cannabis.

Mahmoud is a pleasant fellow with an eager smile and the reckless manner of driving typical of all taxi drivers who run back and forth between Lebanon and Syria. As he blasts forward in what could be construed as a suicide mission he seeks reassurance.

"Driver good?" I tell him yes, he is terrific. About two-thirds of the way through the drive we stop at Lebanon's border where we submit exit cards. A few miles later through a no man's borderland we reach the Syrian crossing and a customs check point.

"Have you been to Israel?" asks the border guard. If we say yes, or if an Israeli stamp appears in our passports, we will be turned away. Travis and I both say no. The guard eyes us with some suspicion. It is the era of the brutal regime of Bashar al-Assad and his minions are everywhere.

In prisons all across the country people are being jailed, tortured, killed. My visa allows me to pass through on the spot, but Travis must undergo thorough and time-consuming scrutiny to obtain a visa for himself, as predicted.

Once we reach the outskirts of Damascus Mahmoud hands us off with a cheerful wave to a taxi driver who will take us into the city, where border drivers like Mahmoud are not allowed. Our cabbie, predictably named Mohammed, takes us on a far less hair-raising ride to the eleven story Cham Palace Hotel. Built in 1983 the Cham Palace looks as though the architect tried to make the place futuristic. Instead it is simply strange, looking like an airport office building, though well located near the city center.

The lobby however, makes up for the hotel's weird exterior, with a hugely high interior, a fabulous gleaming chandelier, a central fountain and loads of comfortable seating. There is something else as well, the alluring aroma of fresh coffee. I check in at the front desk and head to my room, which turns out to be intolerably small.

Returning to the front desk immediately I declare my desire for a much larger room, which I am given on the spot. They probably go through this all the time. The second room is more spacious and far better than the first. I don't even bother to hang my clothes, as there is coffee downstairs, real coffee.

Returning to the lobby I head to a spot where a man at a large table has all the accoutrements of coffee preparation Syrian style. The Arabic method of making coffee here is the same as in Turkey or Greece, starting with finely ground, dark roasted arabica coffee that is thrown into a small hammered copper pot called an ibrik or a dallah, and cooked in water to a frothy boil. It is typically made with finely ground cardamon and sugar, though I ask the lean man making the coffee to hold the sugar. He finds my request strange but complies anyway. After the coffee has reached a foaming boil it is poured through the narrow spout of the ibrik into a small decorative cup called a finjan. He hands me the cup.

The first sip of the coffee is so intensely strong and bitter it almost snaps my head back. I shake my shoulders. The taste in my mouth seems to explode in all directions. One thing is certain, this is real, no-nonsense coffee. I take another tiny sip, which is curiously less bitter than the first, with a slightly sweet undertone. I find that strange.

Taking a seat in a comfortable armchair I examine the impenetrably black coffee, smelling its strong and delightful aroma, taking small sips, letting the flavor linger. It beats the hell out of the Nescafe' at the Summerland and is the strongest coffee I've been served. I take my time and let the cup last. At one point as I sip I come upon the grounds and stop. The sludge at the bottom is thick like mud.

There is a form of divination called caffeomancy, by which the coffee sludge at the bottom of a cup of Arabic coffee is "read," according to patterns made by the grounds. This form of fortune telling is a ritualized process. After the coffee has been drunk a saucer is placed over the cup and the grounds are allowed to settle. Then the saucer-covered cup is turned upside down and the grounds are allowed to settle once more.

The cup is then removed to reveal shapes and forms made by the grounds. Whatever shapes and symbols appear are interpreted according to the insights or caginess of the reader. As willy-nilly as this sounds, the practice is popular and people eagerly lean in to hear what the reader, often an auntie, perceives and has to share.

I already know my future, a second cup. I return to the man at the table and ask for another. This time I am prepared for the head-slamming first sip. Again I sit, lingering over the finjan, savoring the moment. The lobby seems to fade. Sounds around me subside.

The time of day matters not at all. Whatever comes later is not now. This is real coffee reverie of the highest order. I feel that through this experience I am reaching back in time, to the Silk Road and humpy herds of camels laden with sacks of coffee crossing desert sands from faraway lands.

During several days in Damascus this coffee will become a repeatedly sought-after delight, much to the curiosity of Travis, who is a moderate coffee drinker but not equally enchanted by this potent brew. During our daily travels I will repeatedly want to stop for coffee made in this manner.

Eventually wandering the ancient Al-Hamidiyah Souk inside the walled city and beside the Citadel of Damascus on my own I will drink many cups, at one point joining a group of older men who are fascinated that an American is strolling about alone. We will sit and we will speak about many things and we will drink strong amazing coffee. It is a fine way to make new friends.

Chapter 12
Mighty Caffeine

In 1819, a young German analytical chemist named Friedlieb Ferdinand Runge isolated and purified the active stimulant compound caffeine from a small batch of Arabian mokha beans given to him by the famous philosopher and poet Johann Wolfgang von Goethe.

A minister's son, Runge was born in Hamburg in 1794, and earned a doctorate in chemistry from the University of Berlin in 1822. Runge's discovery did not seem monumental at the time, but he had in fact isolated what would become very well known as the world's most beloved and widely consumed stimulant.

Found in coffee, tea, yerba mate, kola nut, cocoa beans, guarana and guayusa tea and many lesser known plants, caffeine is a humble alkaloid also known as 1,3,7 -trimethylxanthine. The alkaloids are ubiquitous throughout nature, and are active compounds in many hundreds of common plants. Some alkaloids are sedative (morphine), some are psychedelic (mescaline), and some possess stimulant properties (ephedrine).

Detected in over 60 plants, caffeine is the most widely consumed alkaloid of all, and imbues coffee beans with the stimulant power to march whole armies and mount global commerce.

"Dream no small dreams for they have no power to move the hearts of men."

-Goethe

Very little caffeine is required produce a stimulant effect. As small an amount as 30 milligrams of caffeine will perk up many, though you can find so-called "energy" drinks that will hammer your central nervous system into a frenzy with several hundred milligrams in one serving.

In green beans, arabica coffee contains 1.1% caffeine by weight, burly robusta weighs in at a hefty 2.2%, and liberica tips the scales at 1.4%. Caffeine is also found in kola nuts (1.5%), tea leaves (3.5%), mate' leaves (1.3%), guarana seeds (3%), and cacao beans (0.1%). These percentages will vary depending on varieties and growing conditions.

The caffeine-bearing plants are widely popular. Whatever contains caffeine will be consumed enthusiastically. This is a maxim upon which you can hang your hat, assured that no philosophical or pseudo-scientific wind will blow it off. Why do we consume caffeine? Because it stimulates us. We love caffeine and we crave it. By stimulating numerous physical and mental functions, caffeine makes us feel very, very good.

Brain and Central Nervous System (CNS) – First and foremost, caffeine stimulates the central nervous system. It is a cortical stimulant, thus mobilizing brain function. It stimulates the flow of blood in the brain, and increases secretion of the important neurotransmitter serotonin in the cerebellum and the cerebral cortex. Caffeine invigorates the mind. It enhances alertness, facilitates thought formation, and decreases fatigue.

- *Cardiovascular system*

Caffeine stimulates the cardiovascular system and increases cardiac output.

- *Renal system*

Caffeine is a mild diuretic.

- *Respiratory system*

Caffeine stimulates respiration.

- *Psychically*

Caffeine inspires the weary, elevates the moderately depressed, and quickens the step of the tired.

How much caffeine?

Look at caffeine tables from coffee industry sources, dietetic databases, hospitals, clinics, scientific papers and commercial propaganda, and you'll find that the numbers differ, often greatly. Differences are due to coffee varieties, amounts of beans used to make coffee, and the roast (light or dark). Here is a brief chart for coffee, compiled from several of the best sources:

Brewed coffee (8 ounces)	80 - 175 milligrams
Drip coffee (8 ounces)	65 – 200 milligrams
Percolated coffee (8 ounces)	40 – 170 milligrams
Instant coffee (8 ounces)	65 - 100 milligrams
Espresso (1 ounce)	30 - 50 milligrams

The caffeine content of coffees varies widely, depending on how much is used, and the method of preparation. Caffeine consumption around the world varies too. Denmark and Sweden win top prizes for consumption of caffeine. They like their coffee strong, and they drink plenty. By contrast, consumption of caffeine in the US is more moderate.

A meta-analysis of caffeine studies performed at the French National Institute of Health and Medical Research, concluded that at around 300 milligrams per day, caffeine improves mood, vigilance, alertness and an overall sense of well-being. Caffeine appears to work on the dopaminergic pathway in the brain, thereby enhancing mood.

For most caffeine tolerant adults, this dosage range produces positive effects. Staying within the 300 milligram range translates into two or three average strength cups of coffee per day. Mayo Clinic offers a somewhat broader range of between 300 – 400 milligrams of caffeine per day for the average adult.

Too much of a good thing

The difference between a medicine and a poison is the dose. You can definitely consume too much caffeine. Negative effects of over-consumption include nervousness, insomnia, and tremors. Excessive caffeine consumption can produce overly rapid heartbeat, mental stress, gastric discomfort and anxiety. The average lethal dose of caffeine for humans is approximately 10 grams, equal to approximately 66 (5-ounce) cups of coffee. Nobody drinks that much coffee. On average, about 15% of people are highly sensitive to caffeine. If you are one of those, you know who you are. If caffeine makes you jittery, sweaty, sick or uncomfortable, then it isn't your substance. For caffeine-intolerant individuals, there is always decaf.

"Decaf is like masturbating with an oven mitt."

-Robin Williams

Caffeine Addiction

In the strictest sense of the term, caffeine is not addictive, but there is no question that caffeine users become dependent upon the alkaloid for a lift. Most caffeine consumers rely on a daily dose, and many get a headache if they do not get their fix of the drug. At first blush, this may seem proof that caffeine is a bad thing. But is this really that much different from relying upon a certain amount of dietary fiber for proper elimination, and getting constipated if you do not have it?

In point of fact, we become contentedly dependent upon many things, including eating regularly, bathing, exercising, sharing the company of others, and attending religious services. One cannot reasonably make the claim that dependence alone indicates harm. It does not. I personally drink on average four large cups of coffee daily, and feel pretty fantastic. Would I prefer to do without? No way. Does coffee in any discernable way put me at any type of a disadvantage? No. Beware of the nattering nabobs who preach the evils of dependency, for we depend on many things to make our lives comfortable.

For Adults Only

Coffee is in my opinion an adults-only substance. Children's bodies are more acutely sensitive than those of adults, and coffee can exert unnecessarily aggressive effects upon their systems. Children consume far too much caffeine in colas and other soft drinks. This consumption can promote restlessness, nervousness, and inability to concentrate. Children do not need to be wired on coffee. All of my recommendations about coffee use and its safety are for adults.

Chapter 13
Chanchamayo Organic 2005

In markets and coffee shops in the US you'll find certified organic Peruvian coffee along with many other coffee varieties from around the world. As with so many consumable products, organic certification is a big deal, and label designations like USDA Organic and Fair Trade matter to an ever-growing sector of the buying public.

Much of the organic Peruvian coffee in the market today comes through La Florida Cooperativa, located in Pichanaqui in the Chanchamayo District of the country's Junin Region on the western slopes of the Andes in central Peru. La Florida is one of several Peruvian organic Fair Trade coffee cooperatives, which include CENFROCAFE, COCLA, APROCCURMA , CECANOR and CECOVASA.

Today about 40% of Peru's total coffee production is located in the Chanchamayo, where growers cultivate premium quality Typica, Bourbon, Caturra, Mundo Nuevo and Villa Lobos varieties of *Coffea arabica*. According to World Coffee Research Peru is the largest exporter of certified organic and Fair Trade coffee in the world. In 2024 Peru's total coffee production for conventional and organic/Fair Trade coffee was forecasted at 4.22 million 60 pound bags.

La Florida Coffee Cooperative, Chanchamayo Peru

Started in 1966 La Florida cooperative has over 820 regional growers who participate in an organic, Fair Trade coffee program that has elevated the region's coffee among the café' cognoscenti and garnered positive reviews from finicky tasters. Offering both green beans and roasted coffee, La Florida provides a better value to regional coffee farmers than the commodity market. They work with the region's Ashaninka and Campa native groups, producing forest-grown coffee backed by strong environmental programs and traceable sustainability.

The cooperative has made a concerted effort to move away from average coffee to supply superior artisanal organic Fair Trade coffee with excellent flavor and aroma. The fertile Chanchamayo soil and steep verdant hillsides, abundant rain and warm days conspire to offer plantations situated 1200 to 1350 meters (3937 to 4430 feet) perfect conditions for superior arabica bean coffee. In doing so they've been able to establish a premium for growers. They sound like an ideal group to visit.

Sergio Cam and I have been on the road in his big red Nissan Trooper for several hours, starting in Lima in the morning. We are headed to La Florida to see for ourselves who they are and what they do. It's a long way to go for what will probably be a short visit, but we roam around a lot and will come up with other places to visit as we go along.

Sergio and I have worked together since 1998 in the maca trade through his group Chakarunas Trading in the Junin plateau and we like to get out into the Andes and the Amazon to explore other botanicals. Plus we both enjoy good coffee. The drive up and over the Andes is long and steep, with traffic and heavily laden mining trucks caroming around blind corners and passing each other in unsafe places, racing at breakneck speed.

All along the road there are numerous tiny little shrines in memory of those who have caromed off the sides of the mountain road to their deaths far below. There are no guard rails to prevent a thousand foot fall. Plus the road is loaded with many dozens of mining trucks carrying gigantic loads of huge rocks. Only good *joss* prevents widespread destruction on the road.

Heading east from Lima on central highway 20 we cruise steadily up into higher elevation, mostly on a narrow two lane paved road. As we climb I notice more vegetation on the hills, and comment on this to Sergio. "It's because this place gets a lot more rain." He replies. As we drive, the air grows cooler and the towns we pass looked less and less like those in Lima. Most buildings are mud and brick, rarely taller than two stories. The hillsides around us get higher, the drops off the sides of the road fall further down, and the switchbacks which zig and zag up into the mountains become steeper. The sky is overcast for almost the whole ride, casting a blanket of gray over the landscape. It is unfamiliar weather for summer.

As we wind our way around the mountains and climb higher, we traverse great grassy valleys that stretch for dozens of miles, many of which afford spectacular views of high, snow-capped Andean peaks. We pass large fields of artichokes and hillsides of opuntia cactus bearing prickly pears. There are large agave in bloom everywhere and San Pedro cactus with large white flowers. At dozens of places, horsetail waterfalls cascade down steep, rocky slopes, rushing into ravines, surging rapidly toward lower elevations.

The Andes, with their snow-capped peaks, are constantly letting off melt water. That perennial condition, plus the bubbling up of springs through fissures in rocks at high elevations, creates a world of streams, brooks, waterfalls, bubbling cascades, vigorous rivers and rivulets, all seeking lower ground. At times, small streams pass right across the road in a pell-mell downward rush.

At one point we see a rock slide, incalculable tons of huge rocks, many as big as cars, slamming and tumbling down a huge mountainside, rumbling like thunder. It is spooky to watch. Sometimes rock slides of that magnitude bury the road we are traveling.

On the way we stop a couple of times to rub our aching kidneys, stretch our compressed spines, and drink coca leaf tea, the national beverage of Peru. The tea, mild in flavor and slightly green in the cup, imparts a tiny amount of naturally-occurring cocaine, which helps to allay the fatiguing effects of thin oxygen at higher altitudes.

The stimulating effect of coca leaf tea is actually less than that of plain tea. More importantly, coca leaf is a rich source of valuable dietary flavonoids and phenols which may protect cells, help to maintain capillary integrity, and enhance heart health. The coca leaf tea proves refreshing and helped us to adjust to the thinner atmosphere as we climbed into greater altitudes. According to altitude acclimation tables we should spend four days reaching the peak of our travels. But nobody does that and we will drive it in less than seven hours.

Higher up in the mountains as we approach Ticlio Pass at 15,807 feet altitude, snow begins to fall heavy and wet, slowing our progress and reducing visibility. The pass marks the highest spot in the central highway connecting Peru's coast to the high Andes and the Amazon. From here it's all downhill for a very long way. The windshield fogs inside, and slushy buildup on the outside taxes the wipers. Sergio runs the palm of a hand against the window to improve visibility. "These conditions are not really that helpful," he notes dryly. After the pass we stop in the grimy copper smelting town of La Oroya for a lunch of rellenos with rice and salsa. The air has a wicked bite to it, conspiring with wind and humidity to make a chilling environment. My field jacket isn't sufficient to keep out the penetrating cold. I add a thick fleece underneath to better retain more body heat.

This ride up and over the Peruvian Andes is not the first of such driving experiences I've had while researching traditional medicines around the world. Whether on the mountain roads of Peru, the Indian Himalaya, or the Chinese mountains of Hunan, many of the places where I hunt medicines have plenty of lousy roads, poor driving conditions, hazardous drops, holes, slides, and huge, rattling vehicles with bald tires, bad brakes, and crazy drivers. It's all part of the mix.

After a couple more hours of travel we descend into Tarma, "La Perla de Los Andes," which is ablaze with acres of colorful fresh flowers for the international floral market. We cruise past the large fruit and vegetable terminal in Tarma, with trucks of produce from all over the Chanchamayo district bustling in and out, and roll on to Rt 20A to San Ramon, La Merced and Perene' before reaching Pichanaqui. The almost ten hour drive has left us tired and hungry. We check into the small and tidy Hospedaje Santa Maria and head right out into the center of town to find Chifa, the ubiquitous Peruvian version of Chinese food.

The next morning after coffee, eggs and toast at a corner restaurant we head to La Florida. Along the way we see some of the cultivation in the area and plenty of coffee growing on hillsides. The

Chanchamayo is a breadbasket farming region with cacao, coffee, oranges, tangelos, mandarins, grapefruit, tangerines, sweet lemons, bananas, pineapples, carambolas, papaya, maracuja and camote. The hills are dotted with farms of all types, most of them a few hectares apiece. Roadside warehouses, truck stalls and depots of various sizes are busy with the agricultural products of the area.

Green Chanchamayo organic coffee beans

La Florida sits right on route 5S, surrounded by a tidy and well-kept wall featuring some of the cooperative's certifications, including Certified Organic OCIA, Naturland, Fair Trade, Max Havelaar, Bird Friendly and several others. It is evident that La Florida operates at a high level of sustainability. Sergio and I enter the gate in the Nissan, parking in a corner of a large open area featuring offices, warehousing, a large cargo track loading sacks of coffee, and about a dozen small plots of drying coffee beans drying in the sun, turned by men and women with large rakes to bring the moisture of the beans down to around 8%. A cheerful man named Manuel comes out of an office to greet us. We explain that we work with plants of all types and are interested in knowing more about La Florida. "I would be happy to show you around," he tells us.

La Florida coffee beans drying in the sun

Over the course of an hour or so Manuel shows us where coffee beans arrive from farms, the drying of coffee outdoors on flat concrete, sorting and grading beans and filling of sacks with coffee beans bearing the La Florida emblem. He explains to us that the business is growing steadily. "More people want organic now. It was hard years ago to get people to care and to pay a premium. But today the market appreciates what we are doing here, conserving land and providing higher value to growers in this area. The cooperative makes coffee a better crop for farmers. Many have only a few acres and can't do well at all in the commodity market." Manuel tells us that their distribution has increased a lot in just the past few years. "many people understand that organic coffee is better all around."

Sorting and grading beans

After our tour I ask Manuel "Where can we get a great cup of La Florida coffee?"

"There are many places, but if you want the very best, go back down the road to La Merced. There is a café' there called Shambari Campa that makes the best coffee in the area, all from our beans. We do a special roast for them. Everybody says it's one of the best cups of coffee they have had. You will be headed back that way, yes? You ask for Mario. Everybody knows him." We affirm that we will need to head back west, and so the 73 km drive to La Merced is no problem. If that's where we can find the best cup of coffee, then that's where we'll go.

Woman raking coffee beans

The drive west back to La Merced takes a little over an hour and a half, by which time Sergio and I are up for a great cup of coffee as promised, and a good lunch. We find Shambari Campa easily and discover that it is a most sought-after destination with an extensive menu and numerous blow-ups of black and white photographs of the Chanchamayo region from the 1800's.

Mario the owner greets us effusively, welcoming us like long lost cousins. When we tell him that Manuel at La Florida recommended his place, he beams with pride and invites us to take a table. "Well yes, we do make the best cup of coffee in this entire area, and I will prove it to you right away."

Sergio and I make sure to put in an order for some food while Mario instructs someone in the kitchen to work coffee magic. Sergio orders lomo saltado and I order pollo con vegetales and fried yucca. Long before the food arrives, Mario brings us two cups of steaming black coffee and sets them down in front of us. "Now you tell me if our reputation is well deserved or not." He takes a seat at the table, waiting for a verdict.

The aroma of the coffee catches my attention first. As steam rises up to my nose the complex aromatic compounds, as many as 1000 of them, tease my olfactory bulb. The coffee smells bright, complex, with hints of citrus and spices. I take a sip. Oh yeah. I look at Mario and give a nod. "Not half bad." Then I laugh out loud. He knows.

"Does our reputation remain intact?" He asks, attempting to look serious.

"This is a great cup of coffee," Sergio comments. We all laugh. Yes it is.

It is an occasion that requires two cups of coffee, fragrant and strong. Fortunately the food takes a while and we are in no hurry. Mario asks us about our work with maca and other botanicals and we tell him about our interest in exploring the Chanchamayo.

"There are some very good traditional healers in this area. You should go to see Rosa Martinez next time, and a fellow named Manuel Harena. They are both very well respected." We promise to do so.

Raking Beans in the sun

90

Our stop at Shambari Campa is the first of many, as Sergio and I will travel around the Chanchamayo region several times over the next few years, meeting local healers, exploring cat's claw, sacha inchi oil, cacao, various fruits and several other botanicals. Each time, no matter what we are doing, we will stop in La Merced to talk with Mario, who will welcome us warmly every time and to drink the very best cup of coffee in the area.

La Florida coffee in sack

Chapter 14
Coffee's Nattering Nabobs of Negativity

As is true for any great celebrity, coffee has always had its detractors. Ever since Khair Bey's short-lived ban on coffee in 1511, the beverage has been criticized by some as injurious to health. Coffee's naysayers have attacked from all sides, coming up with speculative, incorrect and sometimes hilarious ideas about the world's most popular prepared beverage. They have derided its stimulation, warned of its supposed deleterious effects, and spoken ominously of the multitude of ways that coffee supposedly ruins life. Fortunately for coffee drinkers, they are all wrong. For not only is coffee a titan of industry; it is also an agent of great health benefits, as you will learn here.

In a landmark paper published in the May 17 2012 issue of the New England Journal of Medicine, researchers shared their findings from the National Institutes of Health–AARP Diet and Health Study conducted between 1995 and 2008. Following 229,119 men and 173,141 women, Dr Neal Freedman and colleagues found that coffee drinkers who drank at least two or three cups a day were about 10 percent or 15 percent less likely to die *for any reason* during the 13 years of the study. The researchers concluded that "In this large prospective study, coffee consumption was inversely associated with total and cause-specific mortality." In addition, this and other studies have shown reduced risk of cardiovascular disease and type-2 diabetes among coffee drinkers. The message is as clear as a sheet of new glass. If you want to live longer, drink coffee.

On a cool fall day I stood in the humid Victorian-era tropical greenhouse of London's Kew Royal Botanic Gardens, admiring a small stand of lovingly cared-for coffee bushes, of both the arabica and robusta (canephora) varieties. For me, a day at Kew is a day in paradise. Initially a pleasure garden started in 1731 by Britain's Prince Frederick, Kew was established as a botanical garden in 1759 by Princess Augusta and the Earl of Bute.

From that point onward, Kew has developed a collection of plants that is the envy of all other botanical gardens, featuring 300 immaculate acres of greenery by the Thames River. Over the centuries, plant hunters have brought crates of botanical exotica back to Kew from the farthest corners of the globe. Among those who seek new plants, adding one or more to the Kew collection is a badge of honor.

At Kew the coffee plants do not disappoint. Healthy and brilliant green, they show what happens when plants are exceedingly well tended. Kew's scientific staff are leaders in the study of coffee, and have catalogued over 30 species of this plant. I examined the coffee bushes thoughtfully, musing over all the commotion caused by the beans produced from this vibrant plant. Much of the commotion concerned involves bizarre, speculative, and simply half-assed notions of health damage that have no basis in reality.

One oft-repeated myth from the past concerning coffee is that it causes sterility. An account of travels in Persia by Adam Olearius in 1635 describes the effect of coffee "to sterilize nature and extinguish carnal desires." About forty years later, London women, unhappy that their husbands spent more time in the coffeehouses than at home, railed against coffee for taking their men away.

In 1674, a poster printed in London stated the following: "The Women's Petition Against Coffee Representing to publick consideration the grand inconveniences accruing to their SEX from the excessive use of that drying, enfeebling LIQUOR. Presented to the Right Honorable the Keepers of the Liberty of VENUS."

Coffee may have kept husbands away from their homes, wives and beds, but because it stimulated unprecedented conversation and inspired a plethora of fresh ideas, rather than degrading sexual function.

Let us wrestle to the ground the historical claim that coffee promotes sterility, impotence, loss of libido or any other manner of erotic withering. This simply is not so. There is no evidence of any kind that is an effect of coffee.

Coffee does not cool ardor, lower one's staff, defuse seed, nor dry the viscid, lusty juices. Certainly, if you belt down a gallon of potent coffee all at once, you may be too jittery and sweaty to engage in lovemaking. But coffee does no harm to your libido or sexual function. In fairness, some theorists claim that by increasing cortisol in the blood to some extent, coffee can dampen sexual desire. This suggestion is anecdotal, and carries no scientific weight.

Equally, there are claims throughout history that coffee is a sexual stimulant. There is no property of coffee that would likely cause such a reaction, though stimulation of the central nervous system affects the entire body. So perhaps a well-timed cup of coffee could banish the fatigue of a wearying day, and perk you up for amorous activity. Too tired for sex? It's a common complaint. Maybe a coffee lift may help to lift you in other ways. You be the judge. The human brain is the most sensitive of all the sex organs. If you think that coffee will rev up your mojo, then it likely will do exactly that.

One purportedly authoritative paper presented to faculty physicians the University of Marseilles in 1679 declared that burned particles in coffee "sweep along all the lymph...and drain the kidneys." Furthermore, the paper bombastically declared, "the ash contained in coffee induces such persistent wakefulness that the nerve fluid dries up.; when it cannot be replaced, general prostration, paralysis, and impotence ensue."

In 1715 in France, coffee was "proven" to shorten life. Later the beverage was said by physicians to inflame the liver and spleen. The "science" in these cases was spun of vapors. The "proof" was merely fantastic notions repeated until they were presumed true. They were not.

In 1803, the father of homeopathy Samuel Hahnemann fretted in his writings that coffee produced "a wakefulness wrested from nature." He believed that by stimulating the body and dispelling morning grogginess quickly, coffee produced an "artificial sprightliness," and that this was disadvantageous to the human organism. Hahnemann's position was that instead of being pulled from drowsiness by an invigorating cup of coffee, humans were better off slowly climbing out of the nights' slumber unaided. It was a novel theory, if silly and baseless.

Trashing coffee has also helped to sell some alternative products. In 1910, print ads for cereal magnate C.W. Posts' bland-tasting toasted wheat beverage Postum declared "Coffee wrecks some persons." The flamboyant and self-appointed health promoter Post called coffee a "drug drink," and tried to win a large following for his grain-based beverage by scaring people about coffee.

Subsequent to that time, Post developed the popular cereals Grape Nuts and Post Toasties. Since Post's declaration of doom, various health food gurus including Paul Bragg, Gayelord Hauser, Bernard Jensen and nutritionist Paavo Airola, have also eschewed coffee, describing it variously as unhealthful, toxic, poisonous to the system, and on and on. Instead of recommending a fresh cup of coffee upon rising, Airola exhorted adherents of his diet philosophy to take a warm enema instead. His suggestion was lost with the sands of time, while coffee drinking persists unabated. Many critics have gone to great lengths to denigrate coffee as a toxic drink. Yet despite their worrisome claims, coffee consumed in moderation is not associated with any health problems. In fact, the case is exactly the opposite.

"One of my children"

The American Beverage	*versus*	Brazilian Coffee
Raised in America *Millions of Dollars Kept in America*		*Raised in Brazil* *Millions of Dollars Sent to Brazil*
TENDS TO		TENDS TO
Rosy Complexion		Sallow Complexion
Good Digestion		Stomach Troubles
Good Liver		Bad Liver
Good Heart		Heart Palpitation
Peaceful Nerves		Shattered Nerves
Good Flavour		Good Flavour
No Drug		Caffeine, a Drug
Energy		Weakness from Drugging

Try each and judge for yourself.

Instant Postum

Is now furnished in powdered form. A struck teaspoonful stirred in a cup of hot water makes a cup of Postum *instantly.*

"There's a Reason"

Coffee drinkers frequently express guilt over consuming coffee, and many health articles and books rage against this beverage. There is no breach of conduct or offense of any kind committed by drinking coffee. Fanatic food faddists recommend alternative concoctions made of roasted barley and chicory or dandelion as a way to kick a "toxic" coffee addiction. What's next- coffee drinker's anonymous?

Unfortunately, many of the alternative beverages provide pitiably mediocre flavor. If you have tried any of these products, then you know that no matter how well the dandelion root or chicory root is roasted, or how carefully the grains are prepared, these beverages never taste half as delightful as coffee.

For those who have succumbed to the miserable oppression of anti-coffee sentiment, I wish to provide intelligent relief. The anti-coffee movement has made many in the western world pleasure-fearing and fretful. This is a common theme with the pleasures of life, the creeping suspicion if not the outright firm belief that if something feels good, it must be bad somehow, a regrettable habit, possibly even a sin.

Wake up, all you coffee drinkers. Stand united with your steaming cups held proudly aloft. It is now time to push back armed with science and fact. With sober minds let us consider the true lowdown on coffee's effects upon health, without vagary, mumbo-jumbo, fanaticism, knee-jerk reactionary hysteria, deception or pseudo-science.

Chapter 15
Coffee The Health Elixir

Coffee's greatest effects are exerted upon the brain and mind, for coffee is the great, bold awakener. As a caffeinated beverage, coffee stimulates the brain, facilitating cognitive function. Coffee stimulates the flow of blood in the brain and invigorates the mind. It enhances alertness and motivation, facilitates thought formation and concentration, and decreases mental fatigue. Coffee rouses the mental faculties as surely as streaming sunshine and hilarious birdsong awaken the sleeping.

Within a daily dosage range of around 300 – 400 milligrams of caffeine per day, coffee improves negative moods which can occur in the morning upon waking, dispelling the sullen and gloomy clouds which may fog the mind upon rising. Coffee, as the most flavorful and potent caffeine-bearing beverage of all, increases general happiness and feelings of pleasure, and increases positive mood overall.

Coffee promotes an upbeat positive sense of self, and an overall feeling of wellbeing. This is why people love coffee so. Baron Ernst Von Bibra referred to coffee as a "pleasure drug." He hit the nail right on the head. Coffee's reverie is delightful. Simple, easy to prepare, readily available and very fast-acting, coffee makes you feel good. And what's wrong with that? Nothing.

Some purported coffee studies are entirely about caffeine, and not real coffee, which contains in excess of 1,000 compounds, most of which are biologically active. For despite the fact that caffeine is the best known compound in coffee, the protective properties of coffee are actually largely due to a key group of highly beneficial compounds called the chlorogenic acids (CGA).

The chlorogenic acids are an abundant group of polyphenols that include caffeoylquinic, p-coumaroylquinic and feruloyquinic acids. All coffee contains CGA, with robusta or canephora species possessing the highest concentration. CGA are antioxidant and anti-inflammatory and have been very well investigated as protective agents for decades. It is time that researchers stop calling caffeine coffee and consider the whole beverage with its multitude of profoundly beneficial phytochemicals.

"Coffee works a miracle, sharpening the brains of the stupid. No author refreshed thereby need languish in silence. Coffee's strength and virtue double the memory. Every drop empowers us to gabble without pause, and, discarding the crutches of rhyme, to spout fable as history."

- unknown, 18th cent Europe

Plants produce antioxidant substances to protect their cells from premature destruction due to exposure to heat, light, air, moisture, time, bruising, infection and other damaging factors. In the human body, many of these substances and their complex sub-categories are biologically active, helping to protect our cells as well. Furthermore genetic science suggests that these compounds may modify gene activity, enhancing production of our own endogenous protective agents. This health-enhancing modification is known as a nutrigenomic effect.

To simplify, antioxidants inhibit the "rusting" of cells in our body. Just as metals rust due to exposure to oxygen, so too cells in the body become damaged and broken through contact with ROS or reactive oxygen species. These damaging agents, more commonly known as free radicals, are caused by environmental toxins, smoking, poor eating habits, metabolism, exercise and other factors.

When unchecked, free radicals contribute to degenerative diseases. Oxidative damage is associated with diabetes, arthritis, cancer, degenerative brain disorders, and numerous aspects of aging and degeneration.

Over the past several decades, the scientific literature has been flooded with significant studies showing that certain dietary substances contain powerful antioxidant activity that protects cells and reduces the risk of many diseases. In the human diet fruits, vegetables, spices and herbs contain various antioxidants. These include vitamins C, E, beta carotene, and the mineral selenium, phenols, catechins, flavanols, flavonoids and many other classes of compounds. In total thousands of antioxidants from plants are known. Many of these agents are found in coffee, especially the chlorogenic acids, CGA, and antioxidant protection?

Research into the natural chemical properties of coffee shows that the daily brew is a potent protective antioxidant potion that increases healthspan. In this regard especially the chlorogenic acids CGA demonstrate profound protective capacity to protect cells throughout the entire body.

In coffee, CGA rule supreme and co-occur with various other potent antioxidants including caffeine, caffeic acid, cafestol, kahweol, eugenol, gamma-tocopherol, isoeugenol, p-coumaric acid, scopoletin, furans, pyrroles, tannic acid and numerous others. Coffee is notably high in the flavonoid group of antioxidants.

The flavonoids have garnered considerable scientific interest because of their well-studied beneficial effects on human health. In various studies they demonstrate antioxidant, antiviral, anti-allergic, anti-platelet, anti-inflammatory, and antitumor activities.

In fact, coffee is the primary source of beneficial, protective antioxidants in the adult American diet. Most Americans do not each enough antioxidant-rich fresh fruits and vegetables, but they do drink coffee. The bottom line? Coffee protects your body.

The science on coffee as powerfully protective is at this point massive. Interestingly, while coffee roasting diminishes total antioxidant content of green beans to some extent, roasting the beans causes the formation of many other antioxidant compounds not found in green beans. According to some research the average coffee drinker takes in about 420 milligrams of antioxidants from coffee daily, a full battalion of cell protective defense.

Coffee and bones? Caffeine has a negative effect on calcium metabolism. One study has found that women who consume more than 817 milligrams of caffeine per day are at three times greater risk of hip fractures than women who consume no caffeine. But other studies show that moderate consumption of coffee is not associated with any bone loss, increased risk of osteoporosis, or higher rates of bone fractures.

The message of the studies seems clear, that within a moderate range of consumption, coffee has no negative effect upon bone health. Refer back to the recommendation of approximately 300 – 400 milligrams of caffeine per day.

Coffee and cancer? If you worry that drinking coffee is going to result in some form of cancer that will take you down, you can relax. Fears that coffee increases the risk of cancer are completely unfounded. With regard to coffee and its association with other types of cancer, the news is good news. Coffee drinking has been associated with reduced rates of colon, rectal, liver, kidney, ovarian, endometrial and pharyngeal cancers. To the best of my ability to determine, no single factor in the human diet offers as broad anti-cancer protection as coffee, and that is due to a great extent to the chlorogenic acids. Coffee, as the #1 source of dietary antioxidants in the US, offers incomparable anti-cancer protection. Additionally coffee consumption is not known to increase the risk of any type of cancer.

One of the most frequently occurring cancers in the Western world is colorectal cancer (cancer of the colon and rectum). At least three major studies have concluded that drinking coffee significantly lowers the risk of this disease, by as much as 26%. HCC, or hepatocellular carcinoma, is liver cancer. Several studies have shown that the risk of liver cancer decreases with coffee consumption. Drinking 3 – 5 cups of coffee per day is associated with an astonishing 43% lower risk of developing this killer disease.

In the case of ovarian cancer, studies show that drinking coffee has a moderate effect on lowering the risk of this disease. There also appears to be a similar moderate protective effect in reducing the risk of breast cancer as well. So far in the cases of ovarian and breast cancers, the protective activity of coffee is not especially significant.

Pancreatic cancer is almost always a death sentence, and this disease kills in excess of 250,000 people globally each year. While coffee drinking does not seem to provide any significant reduction of risk of pancreatic cancer, it does not contribute to this disease. The same appears true with bladder cancer. Coffee is neither a risk-reducer nor an antagonist.

Regarding skin, coffee drinking appears to exert a protective effect against skin cancers. Drinking six or more cups of coffee a day is associated with as much as a 36% reduction in non-melanoma skin cancers.

Compounds in coffee believed to play roles in its cancer risk-reducing activity include the chlorogenic acids, caffeine, and the diterpenes cafestol and kahweol. Because coffee is a complex substance containing hundreds of compounds, it is hard to know exactly which compounds are responsible for some exact protective effects. But scientific inquiry has concentrated on these agents. When these compounds have been used in concentration in cancer studies, they demonstrate anti-cancer activity. Still, there is a lot more to learn about coffee and its role in cancer prevention. Overall, it appears to reduce risk.

Coffee and cardiovascular health? With cardiovascular disease (CVD) as the leading cause of death worldwide, you certainly don't want to drink something that contributes to this killer disease. The good news is that the majority of coffee studies suggest cardiovascular benefits from coffee drinking, not risks. Antioxidant compounds in coffee exhibit protective power against cardiovascular disease by reducing the oxidation of LDL cholesterol, the so-called bad cholesterol.

By inhibiting oxidation of LDL cholesterol, coffee helps to protect against atherosclerosis, heart attack and stroke. Large population studies suggest that coffee does no harm to the heart, and does not increase the risk of any cardiovascular disease when consumed in moderation. This is even true among individuals who consume six or more cups daily.

Coffee does not raise serum cholesterol when properly prepared. Coffee made by the drip method or by percolation has little or no effect on serum cholesterol levels. However, boiled and unfiltered coffee has been shown to increase cholesterol levels among coffee-drinking individuals in the Netherlands. This is the same method of preparation in "Turkish" coffee, and is a way that coffee is prepared in Syria and other parts of the Middle East. That said, one study of Greek coffee, which is the same as Turkish or Syrian coffee, showed that this method of making coffee improves the integrity of the epithelial lining of the blood vessels.

Your best bet for the heart-healthiest cup is filtered coffee. Nor does coffee elevate blood pressure in regular coffee drinkers if consumed in moderate amounts. Major epidemiological studies show no correlation between coffee consumption and hypertension. The same is true for cardiac arrhythmia. While excessive coffee intake may set the heart fluttering, moderate coffee consumption does not cause irregular or rapid heartbeat.

A major study conducted in Finland concluded that drinking 4 – 5 cups of coffee per day reduced the risk of stroke by 12%. A large study of women found that drinking 2-5 cups of coffee per day reduced the risk of stroke, heart attack and subarachnoid hemorrhage (bleeding in the area between the brain and the thin tissues that cover the brain) by 22-25%. This is a remarkable thing.

The antioxidant components in coffee are also anti-inflammatory. Inflammation is part and parcel of every chronic and degenerative health disorder, including every disease that ends in "itis," which means inflammation. This would include arthritis, nephritis, colitis, and many other diseases. Inflammation is key to diabetes, neurodegenerative disorders, and cardiovascular disease. Agents that are anti-inflammatory help to reduce the risk of chronic degenerative diseases, including cardiovascular disease. Thus the anti-inflammatory activity of coffee may be a primary reason that coffee drinking is associated with reduced rates of CVD.

Coffee and digestion? Coffee exerts well known effects upon the digestive system. Coffee stimulates gastric secretion, and for this reason a cup of coffee after lunch or dinner may be consumed to punctuate and help digest a meal. The morning cup of coffee not only awakens the body and mind, but stimulates bowel activity as well.

A strong cup increases peristalsis, the wave-like motion of the intestines. This stimulates intestinal elimination. Many people rely on a morning coffee for thorough elimination. While coffee shouldn't substitute for a good amount of fiber in a healthy diet, its contribution to proper intestinal elimination is beneficial.

Coffee not only offers welcome laxative activity, but also plays a role in preventing some digestive disorders. Drinking two to three cups of coffee daily can reduce the risk of developing gallstones by as much as 40%. Coffee consumption also shows a strong protective effect against cirrhosis of the liver. Daily intake of 3 to 4 cups of coffee can reduce the risk of cirrhosis by as much as 80%.

Coffee and fertility? Some women feel concern over their consumption of coffee and its effects on fertility and pregnancy, and any possible increased risk of miscarriage or birth defects. Again the news appears to be all good. Most studies do not show any link between coffee and decreased or delayed fertility. There is no evidence of increased risk of miscarriage as a result of moderate coffee consumption, nor any known association with either delayed fetal growth or increased rates of birth defects. In other words, a woman can enjoy coffee daily, and still become pregnant and give birth to a healthy baby.

The American Dietetic Association advises a daily intake of not more that 300 milligrams of caffeine per day as safe in cases of pregnancy. There is no suggestion at this time that a higher intake would cause complications with birth, defects, or birth weight. In at least one major Danish study, reducing caffeine intake during pregnancy did not alter either the length of gestation or birth weight.

All that said, the scenario with massive doses of coffee is quite different. Pregnant lab rats fed the equivalent of 56 to 87 strong cups of coffee per day gave birth to pups with missing toes! As a result of these findings, I must issue a stern warning not to feed the equivalent of 56 or more cups of coffee daily to your pregnant rats. You really have to wonder who comes up with tests like these. Nobody would ever drink such an equivalent amount of coffee.

Coffee and hydration? According to the latest research, concerns about caffeine causing dehydration are specious. There is no reason to avoid coffee in order to maintain adequate hydration. While some people insist that coffee itself does not hydrate the body, this is laughably baseless. Keep in mind that black coffee is more than 95% water. Not one single study shows that coffee does not hydrate. On the contrary, its hydrating properties are well established. Coffee contributes to proper hydration, and coffee drinking contributes to daily fluid intake requirements.

Coffee and mood? As a mood enhancer, coffee is one of the safest and fastest agents on earth. You drink a cup, and blammo- things change rapidly. Surely, this is the primary reason that people drink coffee in the first place. Coffee enhances the flow of blood in the brain, and invigorates the mind. It enhances alertness and motivation decreases mental fatigue. Coffee rouses the mental faculties as surely as streaming sunshine awakens the sleeping. Every coffee drinker has experienced this combination of effects. A morning shower will alleviate grogginess, but a bracing cup of coffee will snap you to attention and prepare you for whatever lies ahead.

In a study published in the Archives of Internal medicine in September 2011, Harvard researchers found that drinking caffeinated coffee lowered rates of depression among women. Women who drank two to three cups of caffeinated coffee a day were 15% less likely to develop depression over the 10-year study period, compared with women who consumed one cup or less per day. Women who drank four or more cups of coffee a day had a 20% lower risk of developing depression. And what about decaf? Women who drank decaf did not experience reduced depression rates. Sadly, decaf drinkers have a higher rate of suicide. Taking one's life is certainly not a consequence of drinking decaf. But going without the mood-brightening benefits of coffee's caffeine can keep a person blue.

Within the previously stated daily dosage range of 300 – 400 milligrams of caffeine per day, coffee improves negative moods which occur in the morning upon waking, lifting the sullen and gloomy clouds which can fog the mind upon rising. Coffee, as the most flavorful and potent caffeine-bearing beverage of all, increases general happiness and feelings of pleasure, and increases positive mood overall. Coffee promotes an upbeat positive sense of self, and a feeling of well-being.

Coffee and neurodegenerative disease - Coffee really does appear to be good for the brain. A number of large population studies show that coffee consumption reduces age-related neurological decline, especially in women. This may be due primarily to caffeine. At least, this is what many researchers believe. People experience accelerated cognitive decline from their 60's on, though evidence suggests that decline may commence as early as age 45.

In cases of age-related cognitive decline, studies on both men and women show that regular lifetime coffee consumption plays a role in stemming decline. Results with women are better than results with men, but in the cases of both sexes, we see better cognitive function in old age among regular coffee drinkers. One Taiwanese study concluded that men and women who do not drink coffee are at significantly higher risk of age-related cognitive decline.

While there are many forms of dementia, between 50 – 70% of those with dementia have Alzheimer's disease. Current research from the National Institute on Aging indicates that the prevalence of Alzheimer's disease doubles every five years beyond age 65.

A majority of studies on coffee and Alzheimer's show reduced risk of developing the disease among coffee drinkers. An especially stunning study found that the risk of Alzheimer's can be reduced by as much as 65% among those who drink 3-5 cups of coffee daily from midlife onward. Caffeine, CGA, and other antioxidants and anti-inflammatory factors in coffee may all play roles in this risk reduction.

Coffee drinking also appears to reduce the risk of Parkinson's Disease. In Parkinson's, motor function slows down, muscles become rigid, gait becomes unnatural, and the production of dopamine, an essential neurotransmitter in the brain decreases. Studies conducted in several countries show that coffee drinking reduces the risk of getting Parkinson's. In one Japanese study, those who drank 4 or more cups of coffee per day were five times less likely to develop the disease than non-coffee drinkers. Subsequent large studies have shown similar protection from coffee drinking. On average, coffee drinkers have between 3 to 6 times lower risk of developing Parkinson's as compared with non-coffee drinkers. The reduction in risk improves as consumption increases from 4 ounces daily to 24 ounces.

Athletes who eschew coffee may think again. In the case of sports, the benefits of coffee seem to be directly related to caffeine. That said, I believe that the glucose-modifying effects of the chlorogenic acids in coffee will eventually be declared valuable to athletes as well, as stable glucose is essential in athletic endeavors.

Coffee appears to be of greatest benefit to those involved in aerobic exercise. Runners, swimmers, cyclists and other endurance sport athletes achieve faster times with coffee in their bodies. This is probably due to caffeine's ability to enhance adrenalin production, improving blood flow to the heart and muscles, and stimulating energy production. According to the European Food Safety Authority, caffeine is best taken by athletes about an hour prior to endurance exercise for best results.

A few studies have shown that caffeine enhances the body's ability to utilize body fat for exercise, and increases the body's ability to work out before fatigue. A cup of coffee before working out can do you good, enhancing both performance and endurance. The International Society of Sports Nutrition issued a lengthy position paper of sports and caffeine, the conclusion of which is that caffeine contributes to enhanced performance, better times, significantly enhanced cognitive performance and superior recovery in athletic activities.

Conclusion - From being the whipping boy of nattering nabobs of negativity who have denigrated it throughout time, to the object of decades of significant scientific study, coffee has proven itself to be a remarkably healthy substance. It energizes, protects, and reduces the risk of killer diseases. Coffee's stimulation is very good for us overall, and its plethora of compounds aid the body in a variety of important ways.

"A cup of coffee is a miracle. A miracle like a musical harmony, a wonderfully compounded assemblage of relationships."

- H.E. Jacobs, Coffee

Chapter 16

The Brawny Beans of Ivory Coast

"People don't make coffee here in Ivory Coast," explains Edouard Fleury at the wheel of a four-seater Toyota pickup truck.

"Instead they drink robusta Nescafe'. It gives you tachycardia. I like the way it makes my heart pound." He knows of which he speaks. Born and raised in Ivory Coast, he has lived there his whole life and runs ITRAD trading company exporting cacao, coffee and other Ivory Coast agricultural products. He also owns and operates two clever pizza restaurants in Abidjan, Pizza Doudou, which operate out of smartly outfitted shipping containers. He is, by his own declaration, the pizza king of West Africa. He also knows the heart-racing coffee of Ivory Coast well, brawny canephora or robusta beans that deliver a whopping load of caffeine and offer a rough flavor experience.

The canephora beans of Ivory Coast are perfect for making soluble coffee brands like Nescafe,' Maxwell House, Starbucks, Mount Hagen, Folgers, Pilon, Juan Valdez and Café' Bustelo. These coffees are made by grinding and brewing roasted coffee beans and then either spray drying or freeze drying the resulting coffee into soluble powder, granules or crystals. Toss a spoonful into a cup or mug, pour in boiling water, stir and you have a rugged cup of strong coffee.

Ivory Coast Coffee harvester

There are some coffee shops in the cities of this country, but otherwise what comes from coffee beans in Ivory Coast is Nescafe', harsh and strong, made in the gargantuan Nescafe' factory that dominates the center of Abidjan. The world's largest instant coffee brand, Nescafe is a colossus. There's almost nowhere you can't find it. I have seen Nescafe' for sale in tiny village stores on remote islands in Vanuatu South Pacific, in a small woodsman's shack on a lonely road in Siberia and up far out rivers in the Amazon. It's the ubiquitous coffee, dark, merciless and heart-pounding.

Coffee plays a prominent role in Ivory Coast. In 1970 the country produced 4.22 million bags of coffee at 60 kg each, at the time the third largest coffee-producing nation in the world. Subsequent political and social instability threw Ivory Coast into turmoil and saw coffee production plunge. In 2024 the country produced 1.4 million 60 kg. bags. Today Ivory Coast ranks number 14 among coffee-producing nations, which still adds up to a lot of coffee. The country's 150,000 coffee farms average about 2.5 hectares in size and grow at between 300 and 400 meters altitude. Almost all the coffee produced in Ivory Coast is canephora, or robusta, with half of the nation's growers belonging to cooperatives.

Canephora coffee tree with ripe cherries

We are headed out of Abidjan along with Axel d'Hauthuille, a work friend and key buyer for French botanical extraction giant Naturex. Axel lived in Ivory Coast as a child, was educated in agricultural engineering in France, and worked for four years managing an Ivory Coast cacao plantation before his years with Naturex. He buys Ivory Coast coffee from Edouard for a green coffee extract product called Svetol, which was originally developed by Berkem, another French botanical extraction outfit. Axel and I have previously traveled together to Morocco and the Peruvian Amazon sourcing botanicals for Naturex. This trip is all about Ivory Coast canephora coffee. It's harvest time November through April so our December trip is ideally timed for seeing harvesters in action.

The fourth man in the truck is Fredericke Wong. Born in Madagascar, he moved to Ivory Coast at age 14. He has worked at ITRAD with Edouard for ten years and knows the various major agricultural products of the country. The four of us are on our way to Man, an area in western Ivory Coast that is the country's largest coffee growing region. We are headed to see for ourselves the large-scale cultivation of canephora coffee by thousands of smallholders in that area. I also imagine that in the heart of coffee production we will be able to enjoy cups of the regional coffee. It only make sense, right?

A few weeks earlier I visited ICO, the International Coffee Organization on Grays Inn Road in London, where the people there graciously allowed me to roam their stacks of books and publications. I was delighted by their hospitality and spent most of a day rummaging through reports, maps, statistics and more. I worked at a table with my laptop and notebooks and gathered as much material as I could for the upcoming trip with Axel.

From the outside ICO looks like many office buildings, nondescript and gray. But inside the shelves of publications in the organization's library hold the keys to the kingdom of coffee. ICO collects and distributes data on the entire world of coffee production and is the epicenter of all coffee information. The many ICO programs, initiatives, conferences and publications help the global coffee industry in numerous ways. In their stacks I read about coffee production in Africa, and found several valuable publications about Ivory Coast and its coffee.

Arabica coffee was first brought to the country by French colonists in the early 1870's, but fared poorly as the conditions for arabica are not favorable there. Canephora or robusta coffee was introduced in the early 1900's and that variety thrived and eventually became dominant in Ivory Coast. The tropical climate of the country, in addition to rich soil and lower growing altitudes make for perfect conditions for that species. With the information I gathered at ICO, an expression of gratitude for the people there and an excellent previously acquired Michelin map of Ivory Coast, I was ready to go.

Small Grower With Drying Coffee

In general the roads in Abidjan aren't so bad. But once you get out onto the highways it is another matter entirely. There are innumerable ways to hurt your vehicle on those roads. Potholes, cracks and fissures in the pavement are ceaseless. Some go completely across the road, so you must navigate with extreme care. Others are so huge they appear to be bombed out. At no time can you get up to speed. Mostly it is necessary to travel under 25 miles per hour.

On the Ivory Coast highways you can burst a tire, deform a wheel rim, break an axle, blow out shock absorbers, snap a spring leaf, destroy tie rods and ball joints and lose mufflers, as evidenced by the copious number of bent and punctured mufflers left for dead on the sides of those roads.

The challenge of travel is magnified at every small town or village, where soldiers with automatic weapons and nothing much to do in the hot, listless sun throw spike strips across the road, demand identification and try to shake you down for money to pass. You don't drive these roads at night when the soldiers have been drinking.

Heading west out of Abidjan on fractured roads we pass rubber plantations with their cups tied to trees filling up with white latex. Huge transport trucks laden with bananas rumble past us.

Everywhere we can see plots of manioc, a common tropical starch food crop, which in Ivory Coast is used to make the popular and delicious fermented dish attieke'. Coffee and cacao and rice trucks rumble past us, groaning and swaying under the weight of huge tonnage. Along the roads women carry baskets of produce and various loads on their heads. In places we roll past teak plantations. We pass squalid, impoverished little villages, meagre encampments and grim markets. There is a tremendous amount of charcoal on display in grubby sacks, as the formerly majestic forests in Ivory Coast are being cut down to make charcoal for cooking.

Axel tells me "Trucks can carry a lot of charcoal, as much as six meters high. Sometimes when they pack the trucks the charcoal is still burning a little, and when the truck gets going in the wind the whole truck catches on fire. It happens about every six months."

Approaching Divo we stop at a small roadside market where women are selling bananas, eggplant, palm oil, papaya, various greens, okra, tomatoes, squash, mung beans and citrus fruits. We roam the market taking photos and speaking with people, and stop at one stand for attieke' and dried fish with salt and hot chiles. Many of the women are happy to have their photos taken and the children are surprised to see us wandering about. When we wave hello and speak to the little ones they giggle and break into big smiles. There is no coffee to drink anywhere in the market.

Slightly further down the road in Divo we stop to see drying cacao and men sorting chaff from the beans. A sign on the wall of a small building designates the place as part of COOPAGARO, a cooperative and member of the Rainforest Alliance. Cacao is the largest crop in Ivory Coast and the country is the world's largest producer and exporter of cocoa beans, with exports at 1.8 million tons in 2023. Everywhere we turn people are doing something with local plants.

Our drive started at 6:00 a.m. and ends at 8:00 p.m. when we pull into a small and lovely lodging outside of Daloa. We find dinner at a local restaurant where several United Nations Toyota Land Cruisers are parked. UN has a peacekeeping presence in Ivory Coast and Land Cruisers are the vehicle of choice for them and for NGO's, having replaced British Land Rovers as the preferred bush vehicles. After a day of banging and bouncing on poor roads sleep cannot come fast enough.

In the morning we enjoy a light breakfast of fruit, toast and eggs, with execrable instant coffee to get us going. Ironically the place where we are staying is only about 200 feet away from a small plantation of Arabusta, an experimental coffee that blends arabica and robusta species in an effort to provide good flavor and adaptability to the Ivory Coast climate and growing conditions.

While Arabusta does grow well in lowland areas, it does not deliver the hoped-for flavor and aroma that its breeders intended. As a blazing orange sun rises over misty coffee-bearing hills we pullout of Daloa, on our way to Man. The roads are better than yesterday and Edouard drives like a man possessed, hurtling through the countryside past pigs, pedestrians, bicycles, numerous cement mosques and odd cemeteries with tombs above ground.

Ripe Ivory Coast Canephora

Man is both a city and also the largest coffee-producing region in Ivory Coast. The area features twenty nine villages and plantations of rice, cacao, plantain bananas and soybeans.

We pull into Douele, as we can see coffee plantations all over the area. We wander around a bit getting curious looks from the locals, and ask a couple of people if anybody they know is currently harvesting coffee. Along the way we take photos of people there, especially some of the local women who are making palm oil from freshly harvest oil palm kernels. "My aunt is harvesting coffee today, I think" answers one man. "I'll take you to her." Just like that we are trooping through the bush, arriving at a place where a woman is strip-harvesting coffee.

While the harvesting of arabica beans is typically performed by making several passes through a plantation to pick coffee cherries when they are red, strip harvesting involves grabbing hold of a coffee branch tightly and pulling your hand toward the branch tip in such a manner as to strip all the beans off whether they are red or green. By this method the beans, along with many leaves and small branch pieces, fall onto tarps and are sorted later on.

Edouard Fleury With Coffee

The woman harvesting coffee is surprised to see us and readily agrees to photos and videos of her working the trees. After we have spent a while with her another man comes along and offers to show us more harvesting. Thanking the woman we have been photographing we set off again through the bush to see more. We arrive at a spot where a lanky young man is also strip harvesting beans. He has a winning smile and is happy to be photographed doing his work. I shoot a few standups explaining what is happening and eventually we thank the young man and set off back to the village.

Harvester With Coffee

We approach a group of men and I ask a simple question. "Does anybody here make coffee?" I assume that somehow I have missed the coffee stops, because we are in coffee country and are surrounded by coffee commerce. But my question appears to be a real stumper. They look at each other and shrug their shoulders.

Coffee Beans Drying In Sun

One man points to a small shack about 300 feet away on a flat area of red earth. "The guy who works there might make coffee." Might? We troop over to the shack and ask the man inside if he will make us some coffee. It is though we have requested tickets to Italy. He gives us a blank look. Edouard explains to him that we have come a long way, that our work here has to do with the local coffee and that we want to drink some. The man looks fabulously unconvinced and reticent, but reluctantly agrees to make some. From a jar on a counter he produces some finely ground beans, throws some into a steel bowl, fills the bowl with water and places that over a burner on a small propane stove.

After a couple of minutes when the water has come to a low boil the man turns off the burner and strains the coffee through an old cloth, into small plastic cups. Edouard, Axel, Fredericke and I each get one. We have come a long way for this cup and it is truly awful.

The aroma is disagreeable and the flavor is so intensely harsh, it's hard to drink. There is no telling how long those ground beans have sat in that jar, oxidizing over months or perhaps years. Nonetheless we soldier through our cups, pay the man more than the little bit he requests, and depart the shack sobered by the experience.

For the remainder of the day we go in and out of small villages where it appears that everybody works with coffee. We see more harvesting, coffee drying in the sun and bagging of beans for sale. There are stacks of coffee under tarps, coffee on jute sacks, and some roasting of coffee in large metal pots over fires.

The people with whom we speak are happy for photographs and express surprise at our interest. We ask them lots of questions about working with coffee and are told that the crop is essential for them to live and eat. Coffee enables them to eke out a poverty wage. It appears that everybody in the area is part of the great world of coffee. At one point we stop at a small village and eat fried plantains and attieke' with hot chiles. We don't ask for another cup of coffee.

119

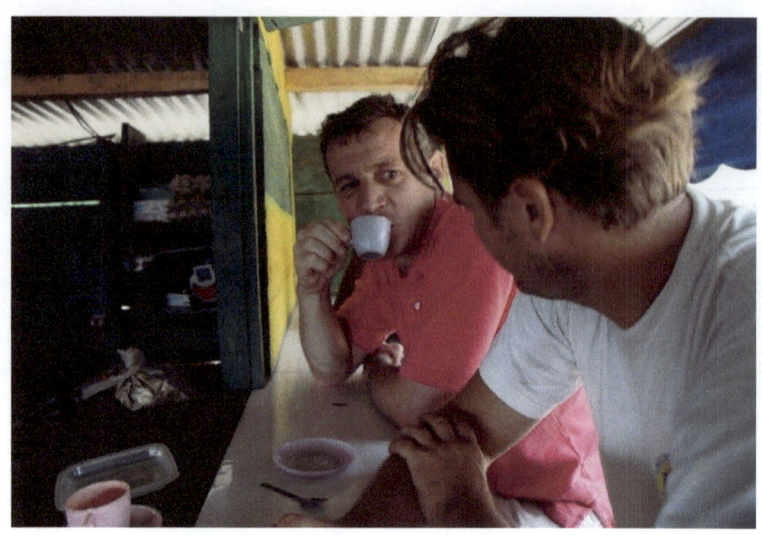

Axel and Edouard with worst coffee ever

Two days after our trip to Man we are back in Abidjan, trail worn and happy to get off the road.

In late morning we visit CAFCO CI, where thousands of tons of coffee are stored for export. The warehouse is close to the giant Nescafe' factory. We walk long warehouse aisles stacked high with coffee sacks, see the lab where beans are graded from 1 – 4 and talk with the managers there about the massive coffee trade. Each sack of coffee in the warehouse reads "Produce of Cote D-Ivoire Coffee Robusta," with the lot number and the grade.

The warehouse handles 25 – 28 thousand tons of robusta beans per year, and is one of many such operations. It is evident from everything we have seen, learned and tasted that in Ivory Coast coffee is a powerful force of nature, a mighty bean with unstoppable power.

Green canephora

Despite the fact that coffee is worth billions of dollars per year and coffee prices are soaring, the farmgate price for growers remains pitiful. In Ivory Coast for the year 2023 farmers received $1.46 per kg (2.2 pounds). At approximately 250 kg of beans per hectare (2.47 acres) and an average plantation size of 2.5 hectares, a farmer makes 912 dollars. This is a poverty wage pure and simple. Nowhere I have been has the poverty side of the coffee trade been so exposed and raw as in Ivory Coast. While people in developed nations spend 3 - $4 on a cup of coffee, in various parts of the world farmers toil in poverty, barely feeding their families. If we wish to live in a humane and just society, it is our obligation to pay a far better wage to those who toil for our pleasures.

Ivory Coast Robusta (Canephora)

Chapter 17

Green Coffee Extract and Chlorogenic Acids

Far afield from drinking an aromatic and flavorful cup of coffee, green coffee extract, rich in the chlorogenic acids CGA, has a place in the nutraceutical field as a supplement for protection of many organ systems. Green coffee extract has emerged over the past twenty years or so as a potent ally in the prevention of a host of health disorders. For overall supplementary bodily protection green coffee extract has few rivals. Scientific studies of CGA show that they offer a multitude of metabolic, cell-protective and system-regulating benefits, helping to stem many diseases and extend lifespan. These benefits are so significant and well-substantiated that in the nutraceutical market, concentrated extracts of green coffee beans high in CGA, such as the extract Kaffanol are popular as protective supplements.

As you have read previously, before coffee beans are roasted they are green. This is their natural color. Green coffee beans are waxy and hard, and possess no interesting aroma or flavor. The fermentation and roasting of coffee beans transforms them and makes them suitable for the preparation of a cup of coffee. But fermentation and roasting reduce somewhat the concentration of antioxidant agents in coffee, including a greater concentration of active principles in plant material for extraction results in a higher yield of these compounds and greater efficiency of extraction.

To define terms, I'll explain what is an extract. As it applies to plants, this is any and all soluble material that has been removed from the cellulose "skeleton" of plants using a solvent of some kind. The physical body of plants is made of cellulose, an inert substance. Within the cell walls of cellulose, plants contain many hundreds of compounds. An extract of a plant is all those compounds without the inert cellulose.

The most relevant example of an extract for our purposes is a cup of coffee. When you grind coffee beans and pour water over them, the resulting fluid is an extract. The solids of the coffee, known as grounds, are left behind and the fluid remains. This is the same process by which a cup of tea is made. There are many forms of extraction. When this is performed on a large industrial scale for the purpose of creating extracts for the nutraceutical market, solvents may include water, alcohol, or even other agents like acetone or hexane or methanol. My personal position is that water and pure alcohol (ethanol) are safe extraction solvents, and anything else, with the exception of pure carbon dioxide, should not be used, due to toxicity of the materials. Instant coffee, generally made from robusta beans, is an excellent example of a concentrated, chlorogenic acid-rich extract. It also enjoys solubility, dissolving very well in hot water.

The manufacture of green coffee extract starts with raw, green robusta aka canephora coffee beans. These beans are placed into huge stainless steel tanks, into which water and alcohol are added. Under pressure, the coffee beans are "cooked' in the alcohol and water solution, until the soluble compounds have been completely extracted. The inert solid material of the coffee beans is discarded. From there the fluid extract of green coffee is evaporated, concentrated, dried and made into a powder. This simple-sounding process is actually highly technical, performed on a large multi-ton industrial scale, in special facilities designed solely for this purpose.

A substantive body of scientific literature shows that green coffee extract acts directly upon the body in ways that regulate blood sugar, cause the body to use stored fat for energy thereby reducing body fat to a moderate extent, and help to control various parameters of metabolic syndrome. Legitimate green coffee extracts contain 45-50% chlorogenic acids, of which 10-15% is the specific chlorogenic acid known as 5-caffeoylquinic acid. Investigations of these extracts and their absorption, safety and health benefits have been undertaken since 2000. If you are trying to control your blood sugar, gradually reduce overall body weight and stabilize other factors like high triglycerides, green coffee extract can help with that. CGA intake is directly correlated with improved metabolic balance, healthier body mass, lower triglycerides and more stable blood sugar. Other factors, such as dietary control, exercise and eliminating processed foods and reducing alcohol consumption are all important parts of the metabolic health package. There is after all no magic bullet for health.

Green coffee extract is not a weight loss miracle, though it has been marketed as such. In human studies of people who consume green coffee extract some lose weight very slowly, a pound or so every two weeks. This is not the kind of weight control featured on magazines at supermarket checkout counters with headlines that boast of huge weight loss in short periods of time. Those headlines are simply fantasy. For while incremental weight loss is possible with green coffee extracts, virtually all of the large studies investigating these extracts show that this effect is far from settled. Without accompanying lifestyle changes in diet and exercise the results are negligible.

Not everybody drinks coffee. But both those who do and do not drink coffee may want increased overall protection to enhance healthspan and reduce the risk of degenerative diseases. Green coffee extract, with its high value of CGA can greatly add to your body's defense against factors that deteriorate health. As such it is a valuable aid in maintaining better quality of life.

Chapter 18
A Congo Sighting 2014

Around Kisangani, formerly Stanleyville the capitol of Tshopo Province in Democratic Republic of Congo, six of us are visiting various wild places and experts who know many of the hundreds of medicinal plants of that biodiverse region. Our generous host Jerome Lippens has provided us with a Beechcraft King Air – the Bentley of the skies – and two seasoned pilots Paul and Jeff, who have flown all over the African continent for decades and have entertaining stories about narrow scrapes with danger and sketchy landings in rough places. It is extraordinarily privileged travel, juxtaposed with the crushing poverty, high crime and overall social and political instability of Congo itself.

Full moon over Congo River

After a visit to the dilapidated but formerly splendid botanical gardens in impoverished Kisangani, my travel partners Jerome, Anant, Brieuc, Francois, Jean and I set off southeast of the mighty Congo river in SUV's with drivers who are also big muscular armed guards, to Mbiye Island.

The 31 kilometer long island on the Lualaba river features dense protected rainforest as part of a Congolese forest management program. The Congolese forests are legendary for their biodiversity of flora and fauna though they are being cut down and rapidly destroyed. It is a familiar story all over the world, vast rainforests cut down for timber, cattle grazing, minerals and development.

Africa is a resource-rich continent in turmoil and flux at all times, and Democratic Republic of Congo aka DRC is among the least safe places to travel. Thus we move about at all times with bodyguards in heavy duty vehicles. We drive along undeveloped roads until we arrive at a small cluster of simple huts. Parking there we meet a couple of local guides who have been waiting for us. Leaving the SUV's and guards behind, we follow the guides along a narrow path into the bush, hiking a path for some time, eventually arriving at a large swamp.

To cross the swamp we all get into a long and shallow boat carved from a single narrow log. Standing in a line and balanced precariously we slowly glide along in the swamp as guides wade beside us pushing and stabilizing the boat. A little more than halfway across, one of the guides says "okay." Okay? With hand gestures he indicates that we are to get out of the boat and go on a few hundred yards through thigh-high water. I wonder why we bothered with the boat.

I turn to Ananth "Are there black mambas in here?" referring to one of the deadliest snakes on earth the African *Dendroaspis polylepis*, a large, fast and aggressive serpent. Untreated black mamba bites have a 100% mortality rate. Best to steer clear of them.

"Yes." He answers stiffly. Well that's not reassuring. We slog along in black waters, eventually reaching shore where we spend several minutes ridding ourselves of leeches, carefully removing the parasitic worms from our legs and arms.

The leeches are very fast setting up shop and some have made it up to our thighs inside our pants. I produce a sharp folding knife, as I have learned from experience that shaving leeches off with a blade is a quick way to get rid of the wriggling blood-suckers.

Once we are relieved of the leeches we head off through a long stretch of razor grass that leaves us each with dozens of tiny red cuts on our arms and necks. Eventually we enter dense forest where the foliage is thick, the trees are high and the sun is largely blotted out. The 90F heat combined with heavy humidity and the closeness of the forest makes a sweltering combination.

All rainforests are different one from another, due to their locations, types of flora and fauna, weather conditions and more. This forest is dark, dense, heavy green, mysterious, unfamiliar. Our guides hack along with machetes, clearing a path. It is slow going.

The smells are rich and deep. Small groups of butterflies erupt from little spots here and there. Lizards scamper on trees. We spot monkeys in high tree tops. There is a magical quality to this place. As we hike through forest we spot a number of medicinal plants including the broadly beneficial and decorative *Tetradenia riparia*, the small *Aloe Congolensis* and the purported sex-enhancers *Mondia whitei* and *Scorodophleus zenkeri*.

In most places it is impossible to see the tree tops. Frogs croak, monkeys hoot and parrots squawk as we make our way deeper into the woods. We spend a couple of hours in the forest as our guides familiarize us with this grand and ancient place. They tell us sadly that poachers regularly take animals from this forest to sell as bush meat along the regional roads.

A couple of hours later back at our little security compound hotel in Kisangani Les Chalets, we hang by an unappealing and milky pool before dinner. Prostitutes sit sipping colas in leafy shadows waiting for business and I get into a long conversation with Paul the pilot, who has been flying for 30 years and shares some of his escapades and narrow scrapes in Africa. We eventually eat dinner and settle in for the evening after beers and conversation.

The next day we set off again in the SUV's, this time for a long drive on red dirt roads far into the Congolese countryside north of Kisangani. During the rainy season October to May these roads are often impassible. We ride through miles of deep green forest to a faraway botanical research station that turns out to be a small green hut in a tiny impoverished village. A crowd of children run to greet us. There we meet a couple of local botanists who are thrilled that we have come.

After brief introductions we set off on a small path that leads into dense dark forest. Along the way the local botanists point out various medicinal trees, shrubs and other plants. The smells of the forest are heavy, musky. For an hour or so we hike deeper into the forest, following a path that had been cleared previously, making our passage easy.

Plant hunters lunch in forest

We have brought a sack of sandwiches made for us at Les Chalets, with extras for the botanists. Finding a small clearing in the forest we sit on the leafy ground and share them with our new friends, surrounded by the sights and sounds of wild Congo. Insects chirp and buzz and hum and mosquitoes attack at every opportunity. After we finish our sandwiches we continue our hike. That's when I spot a wild *Coffea canephora* tree with a few red cherries. It's an exciting moment.

Congo has among the greatest diversity of wild coffee anywhere in the world, with several wild lineages suitable for cultivation on a mass scale. In 1898 Belgian colonists discovered wild *canephora* (robusta) coffee in Congo and that kickstarted commercial coffee production in the country. *Coffeea canephora* originates from the forests of Congo and coffee research and breeding programs around the tropics have relied heavily on the hardy genetics of *canephora* from the Congolese forest for commercial development.

Among more than 94 genetic lines discovered throughout Congo, seven in particular have proven excellent for breeding. In Congo an estimated 800,000 households are involved in coffee production. Congolese strains have been exported to Java, Vietnam, Brazil, Uganda, Ivory Coast and India where they have been cultivated over vast acreage.

Today Vietnam is the second largest coffee-producing nation in the world after Brazil, almost all of it *canephora* originating from Congo. More robust and environmentally adaptable than *arabica* with double the caffeine and richer in many biologically active constituents like the chlorogenic acids, *canephora* represents around 40% of global production and is the reigning species for soluble coffee and canned grinds and a staple at late night truck stops and diners.

Wild Coffea canephora

We pick a few wild coffee cherries, pop them into our mouths and break the fruit with our teeth to reveal the succulent sweet membrane inside. I marvel to myself that we are standing in the heart of coffee's earliest history, that *canephora* coffee originated from these dark forests, and that we are enjoying sight and taste of the primordial origins of coffee. It is a magnificent moment. We take photos all around and laugh excitedly. I should have said Eureka.

Congolese Coffea canephora

Eventually we turn around for the hike back to the village. At one point we come upon an unavoidable wide swath of fierce teeming ants, many of which leap upon us, scramble up our pant legs and bite the hell out of us, leaving angry welts. The Congolese ants are brutes and convey a searing bite.

Back in the little village I spend about an hour photographing children who marvel and laugh at themselves on the camera's digital display. They are endlessly entertained. It is a beautiful way to conclude a most excellent day in the deep forest of Congo.

Chris Kilham With Congolese Children

Chapter 19
Vietnam's Zen Coffee 2024

"For humanity, coffee is not just a staple drink, but also no less a source of nourishment for the mind."

Trung Nguyen Legend

As we descend into the airport at Buon Ma Thuo in Vietnam's Dak Lak province, the speakers on our VietJet blast the patriotic song "Ballad of Ho Chi Minh," a paean to the country's former president and founder of the Socialist Republic of Vietnam, also known as Uncle Ho. The rousing ballad, released by Scottish singer Ewan McColl in 1954, praises the virtues and courage of the leader who led Vietnam through what Americans refer to as the Vietnam war, and what the Vietnamese know as the American war.

"From Viet Bac to the Saigon Delta
Marched the armies of Viet Minh
And the wind stirs the banners of the Indochinese people
Peace and freedom and Ho Chi Minh."

– Ballad of Ho Chi Minh

The triumphant anthem, with its stirring and patriotic lyrics, blares throughout the jet cabin. In many ways it is the ideal send-off into a land of supercharged, energizing canephora coffee. For Vietnam is not just another tropical stop along the coffee belt. Behind Brazil Vietnam is the second largest producer of coffee in the world, most of it canephora. There is a fierce coffee pride in the country and a determination to be known far and wide as one of the three great coffee cultures, and the center of "zen coffee."

"The Ottoman coffee culture originated from the cultural traditions of Ethiopia, the birthplace of coffee, as well as Turkey and other countries across the Middle East.; Roman coffee culture stemmed from the cultural traditions in Italy, as well as in other countries in Europe, including France, Germany and Austria; And the flow of Vietnamese culture, which resonates with pottery and bronze drums, are combined with the aesthetics of the Japanese tea ceremony, inspiring the creation of the Zen coffee culture." – World Coffee Museum, Buon Ma Thuot, Dak Lak

Antique coffee cart *World Coffee Museum*

My work mate Nebil Bourguiba and I are here on behalf of French botanical extraction company Berkem, maker of a green coffee extract from robusta beans. Nebil has found a company who has a well-defined sustainability program and who can also supply tonnage of green robusta coffee beans. Helena Coffee is the kind of source we seek, well-established and dedicated to environmental and cultural sustainability. Their slogan is "together make a better world." In the rough and highly competitive world of coffee, better wages for coffee workers and improved care for the environment matter greatly, as the global impact of coffee production is immense.

"If you want to improve your understanding, drink coffee."

– Sydney Smith

Canephora plantation row

Dak Lak province is Vietnam's largest coffee growing region, with approximately 213,300 hectares of coffee cultivation and an annual output exceeding 526,000 tons, accounting for over one third of the country's total coffee production.

The conditions here are usually ideal for coffee, with an average annual daily temperature of 24C or 75F, abundant rain and average humidity of 81%. But drought in 2023 harmed coffee and reduced total production in Dak Lak by as much as 20%. For farmers it was a very hard time. As with every crop, weather can make or break success. Approximately 220,000 households are supported by Dak Lak coffee production, so a negative impact of that size and scale is hard on whole communities. Everybody feels the squeeze. At the same time, domestic demand for Vietnamese coffee is on the rise, creating both more opportunity and more pressure on growers.

Green canephora

Vietnam has transformed from a tea-based culture to a coffee-based culture and in urban areas you see coffee shops on every side of every block on every street. In the Dak Lak capital of Buon Ma Thuot, high signs bridging major roads feature plaques of coffee beans, making it clear that in Dak Lak coffee is king. Currently Vietnamese coffee from Dak Lak, which is known as the highest quality coffee in Vietnam, exports to over 13 countries, and big names like Starbucks, Caribou, Lavazza, Tully's and many more buy from the region.

Nebil and I make our way to the offices of Helena Coffee in Buon Ma Thuot, where we are greeted by Ben (Le Ba Hai) and Edison (An Nguyen), the company's co-founders. There we are treated to a full coffee experience, with a coffee educational center, coffee roasting, and a lab investigating the various properties of coffee. Charts and graphs on the walls describe some of the many hundreds of compounds in coffee, and the various hundreds of aromas that can emerge with roasting.

A medium size roaster dominates a corner of the educational room and coffee making accoutrements line up on a counter. Whether you want a cup of drip coffee or an espresso, it can be made here. I ask for an espresso and in no time at all a young woman named Quen serves me a canephora espresso so intense it nearly knocks my teeth out. This is Vietnam, land of canephora, where coffee is imponderably strong and dark and no amount of milk or cream or even heavy condensed milk can lighten the inky black drink.

At the end of its journey through the marketplace coffee commands a very high price for a small amount of beans. Specialty coffees can sell for big dollars per pound and coffee drinks are inexpensive to make yet sell for many dollars per cup. Meanwhile growers and harvesters eke out a living at the whim of market fluctuations, receiving the lowest economic benefits of anybody along the chain of coffee trade. Sometimes they give up the poor money of coffee production and move on to durian plantations or doing some logging, whatever it takes to feed a family.

Nebil with coffee seedlings

At the same time around the world a great many sustainable coffee projects are elevating what has always been a low or even poverty wage industry for growers and harvesters. The previously mentioned La Florida is a good example. By bringing growers together they exert greater market power and can help with improved pricing and production standards including drying, cleaning, sorting, grading and marketing. Organic and Fair Trade certifications help to lift small plantations out of the lowest rung of the commodity market and help coffees to become sought-after varieties. There is a growing market for coffee that tastes great and is sustainably produced. Single origin coffees, coming from just one plantation, have broken through into the coffee market and are in high demand, just like wines from one vineyard or tequila from one hacienda. The world of coffee is changing and the market likes variety.

"Without my morning coffee, I'm just like a a dried-up piece of roast goat."

– Johann Sebastian Bach

Helena is one of those enterprises elevating the coffee game. Ben and Edwin gave us a rundown on the company's mission. Started in 2016 Helena Coffee has grown into one of the larger coffee production and export operations in Vietnam, supplying both canephora and arabica coffees to places far and wide including the United Sates, Thailand, China, Singapore and many more nations.

The domestic market is significant as well and Ben focuses his attention and efforts on that sector. Even though Vietnam is mostly a canephora-producing nation, there is some arabica growing in the highlands and this is part of Helena's portfolio. Helping farmers to improve quality of coffee production, encouraging organic and fair wage practices and providing better market access for producers is all part of their ongoing efforts to deliver premium coffees to the global market. Unlike what I saw in Ivory Coast where the stripping method of harvesting takes green and red cherries alike, Helena insists that only red ripe cherries are picked, to ensure full maturity of the beans inside.

At the time of our visit Helena was selling 10,000 tons of canephora and 5,000 tons of arabica per year. Both Ben and Edwin are determined to see those figures grow greatly as the company expands its efforts. Edwin explains "Because of our fair wage practices we cannot compete with prices in the commodity coffee market, so we turn to the specialty coffee sector where this is appreciated and our prices are competitive."

Nebil and I like what we hear and know that we'll learn a lot by investigating one or more of the plantations operated by Helena. There is no substitute for getting into the field and seeing as much of operations as possible. Around dinner time he and I head off to Arul House, a remarkable restaurant and café' featuring old Vietnamese artifacts, a traditional longhouse for sitting, a hip decor and amazing food and coffee. The coffee is so good there it's promoted on several Vietnam coffee websites. We discuss the day, have a fabulous meal and prepare for a trip to a large coffee plantation in the morning.

Drip coffee

Edison, Quen, another woman from Helena and a driver named Loi pick us up in the morning at our hotel and whisk us off to a relatively nearby plantation, the Eakmat Coffee Research and Technology Transfer Center. A key aspect of the center's activities is to develop superior fertilizers for maximum healthy growth and yields of coffee trees, and to transfer that knowledge and products to regional growers.

The center also supplies seeds and seedlings to farmers. Along the way we see signs for coffee wholesalers, coffee seedling nurseries, coffee shipping. The plantation, established in 2018, appears healthy and neatly tended.

The trees are tall and slim with shiny bright green leaves and abundant red cherries ready to pick. We each pluck some, pop them into our mouths, crack open the flesh and suck on the sweet mucilage-covered beans. In a coffee plantation everybody does that, as the covering around the beans is delicious and floral/fruity. There is also plenty of leaf litter around, which is typical. You must always be careful of piles of leaf litter and stay on well-trod paths, as these leaves may hide various cobras, kraits and pit vipers, several of them fatally poisonous.

According to WHO as many as 138,000 people die from poisonous snake bites each year, with a greater concentration of them among poor people in agricultural areas of Asia and Africa in fields and forests where people work with various crops of all types, from timber to roots to fruits. An additional 400,000 people annually incur disabilities including amputated limbs as a result of snake bites. It is a significant hazard.

After visiting the Eakmat coffee plantation we move on to the Nescafe' WASI (Western Highlands Agriculture & Forestry Science Institute) Coffee Farm Experience Center on the outskirts of Buon Ma Thuot. If there is a burnished jewel of coffee research and education in Dak Lak, this is it. The 100 hectare research plantation of robusta coffee is very nicely cared for and monitored for maximum yield per tree per acre and overall health of the plantation.

The coffee trees are in excellent shape and the grounds are well tended. Wide, well raked paths run through the entire plantation. Nestle can afford to dedicate resources to this research center and the information they garner, to benefit Dak Lak coffee producers.

Nestle coffee plantation

Opened in 2011 the Coffee Farm Experience Center center features a modern two story building with a prominent Nescafe' logo. The first floor offers an educational experience for visitors, who can learn about the cultivation and processing of coffee from seedling to harvest and to sample coffee at the end.

The second floor offers a more relaxed environment with coffee from nearby growers and some food. Helena contributes time and coffee to this effort. This connection between visitors and farmers helps to establish a better understanding of the world of coffee in Vietnam, promoting sustainable development and increasing the value of Vietnamese canephora coffee globally. Visitors can freely wander the manicured plantation, observing various stages of coffee growth and harvesting in season, typically starting in November.

A major aspect of Nestle's mission with the center is to develop and implement methods for improved coffee farming and processing, to continually elevate Vietnam coffee. Nestle and WASI together have supplied large numbers of Vietnamese farmers with the TRS1 large bean and high yield variety of drought and rust-resistant canephora coffee seeds and seedlings, making that cultivar the dominant replanting coffee in Dak Lak. Over 80% of coffee grown in the Central Highlands of Dak Lak now comes from varieties researched and developed by WASI.

As the second largest coffee-producing nation in the world, Vietnam must constantly innovate and upgrade all aspects of coffee production, from irrigation to fertilization, the development of high-yield varieties and more, to maintain not only a high volume market but one increasingly known for good quality.

Canephora beans will never replace arabica beans for flavor and aroma, but all aspects of the country's coffee can still be advanced to produce a better product and to garner greater traction in the specialty coffee market. What Nestle learns in its 100 hectare plantation gets translated into sustainable practices taught by extension experts through courses, training manuals and field initiatives. It is nothing less than a full-on effort to move Vietnam to center stage in the highly competitive world of coffee. What gets learned here also translates into improvements in Nescafe itself, creating a more satisfying experience for that soluble coffee's drinkers.

In Nestle coffee plantation

Later in the day Nebil and I tour the World Coffee Museum in Buon Ma Thuot, where we see a large number of implements and appliances used in the coffee trade and learn about the development of coffee in Vietnam. I order an espresso at the museum coffee bar and it is strong but pleasing.

Trung Nguyen Legend, the country's largest coffee producer, has invested heavily in the museum and plays a role in providing education and history about Vietnam coffee. The museum promotes zen coffee, which not only involves non-hurried coffee preparation, but also fosters attentive and relaxed enjoyment of coffee for a clear and energized mind.

"Coffee is a treasure of the universe, a heritage of mankind and a solution for the future."

– Dang Le Nguyen Vu

The next day after breakfast at our hotel Muong Thanh and muscular coffee that makes my heart pound like a trip-hammer we are again greeted early in the morning by the same crew, this time for a one hour journey to Helena's largest coffee plantation, a 450 hectare robusta farm north of Buon Ma Thuot in Chu Kbo, in the rural central highland district of Krong Buk. The region features over 20,560 hectares of coffee, and along the way we see shops and offices for seedling growers, processors, shippers and various traders as we head to Helena's plantation. Edison has talked up the plantation a lot and so we expect to see something splendid.

Edwin at Helena robusta farm

When we arrive at the Helena Robusta Farms, a dog barks at us ferociously but only for a minute or so. Then it wanders back to shade and appears to forget about us. Thus far the watchdogs we have encountered seem somewhat desultory. They do their part to bark and make noise, but seem to tire of watchdog duty quickly. From the road we can see that the many thousands of coffee trees go way down a large hill and all around a big pond, covering a large amount of land.

The trees are beautiful green and show no signs of decay, rust or other visible problems. Nebil and I had hoped to see harvesting in full swing but we are a good month early and so only a few red cherries appear on the trees. A profusion of elliptical green cherries suggest a good yield. The farm, which lies at 850 meters, produces between 800 – 1000 tons of coffee per year. This is not like the mostly 2.5 hectare coffee farms that make up the majority of Vietnam's coffee production. Instead this is a much larger commercial venture.

Green coffee cherries

Edison's uncle Duon joins us from the house where the indifferent watch dog lives and offers to show us some harvesting. He manages the farm, which was started by Edison's father in the 1990's. "There are enough red cherries that I can show you." He has a woven basket and a wide hat to cover him from the increasingly broiling sun. We follow Duan down a long lane between coffee trees until he spots one with red cherries.

"We only pick coffee when it is ripe and ready, not before," Edison says. "This plantation will be all red in another month or so. Then we will have many harvesters out here. Right now it is relatively quiet." As Edison points to the numerous heavily-laden trees around us, Duon picks red cherries while Nebil and I take photos. After we watch Duon for a while I head off on a long stroll through the plantation. There are times in a coffee farm when there is nobody else around, when the coffee leaves glisten in the sun and birds chirp all around, when the sun presses down with high heat and insects buzz. I wander the wider lanes between rows and make my way down to the pond.

The air is fresh and clean. I feel a kinship with the coffee, a plant that has wooed me and tantalized my imagination for decades. From there I wander off in a lateral direction, traversing other paths in the reddish-brown earth. For the most part the paths are well cleared. I see no snakes during my walkabout.

Harvesting ripe robusta

"This place is pretty great," Nebil tells me when I return to the road and our van. "I think they can be a good source for us." I agree. Between the company's sustainability initiatives and their high level of production, it looks as though in Helena we have found a right supplier for green robust beans to extract.

After another hour or more of wandering the plantation and photographing beautiful coffee trees it's time to leave. As we open up the van windows and doors and prepare to depart, the watch dog stands up as though to bark at us. But after a minute it wanders back off into shade and that is the end of its interest in us.

Ripe Vietnam canephora

In viewing various coffee sites and spending time with the people at Helena Coffee, we have a good sense of the Vietnam coffee market. It is large, well run and vibrant. Vietnamese are proud of their coffee. From humble plantings in the late 1800's to now, Vietnam has forged ahead with the noble bean, determined to deliver the country into the highest realms of commerce, and ardently devoted to the greatest invigorating beverage on earth.

Vietnam barista

Coffee sack

Chapter 20
Saving Coffee From Extinction

Perhaps the constant flow of bad information about global climate change and its devastating effects has become only too common a background theme for daily life. Maybe the steady deterioration of the Great Barrier Reef seems just too far away, the ongoing loss of trees in Borneo too overwhelming, the rapid devastation of the Amazon rainforest and its life too sad to dwell upon. But maybe, just maybe, the fact that global climate change is adversely affecting coffee production may make you stand up and pay greater notice. Yes, for real, your cup could run dry. Climate change is hurting coffee. I have seen the signs.

Articles in major media talk about farmers struggling to produce enough coffee to earn a living. Trees are producing lower volumes of beans. Per acre yield is down. A bag of coffee used to be one pound. Then for several years it was 12 ounces. The other day I noticed that many bags are now 10 ounces. And the price? It is going up.

Enter Dr. Aaron Davis, a very busy man. As Head of Crops and Global Change for the venerable Kew Royal Botanic Gardens outside of London he assesses the impact of global climate change on various food crops of all types. And as Head of Coffee Research he is on a mission that potentially affects many of us, working to save coffee from extinction. He works in the field, notably in Ethiopia, Uganda and Sudan, writes papers, and speaks at conferences on the need for new species of coffee to replace current species that don't stand up well to increased temperatures. I had read his latest paper *High extinction risk for wild coffee species and implications for coffee sector sustainability*, and determined that this was a climate change issue that just might sound a more personal alarm than the loss of fragile types of moss in polar regions. After all, this is coffee we are talking about, the world's most ardently desired and healthiest beverage after water.

On a February day that felt like spring I sat with Aaron in his office at Kew, a room filled with books, papers, and numerable accoutrements of coffee making. Outside crocuses were already in bloom and Kew staff members were tearing up dead plants and planting new ones, raking the detritus from winter and helping to maintain the splendor so characteristic of the world's greatest and most venerated botanical garden.

"Changes in global temperature are reducing the productivity of coffee trees in most areas, including Ethiopia, Brazil, Vietnam and many other coffee growing regions," he explains. This can be devastating to small growers all over, and to everyone in the coffee sector. Coffee production is declining, prices are going up, and we must prepare for the future."

My mind operates on two tracks. While Davis is spelling out how coffee production is down in areas where Arabica coffee grows, I am casting a look about his office, noting the various coffee appliances – a desktop roaster, a burr grinder, a Lucite Aero Press coffee press, a scale for weighing beans, a French press, a hot water pot, cups, filters. I ask Aaron if he knows James Hoffman, a barista champion, author, founder of London's Square Mile Roasters and YouTube superstar whose coffee videos are highly popular and much admired. "We're good friends," he replies. Of course. In the empyrean of the coffee greats, Hoffman and Davis stand among the royals. Hoffman is bent on the perfect cup, and Davis is working hard in the tropics to keep that coffee flowing.

With over 125 million growers globally between the tropics of Cancer and Capricorn, coffee is a monster crop serving up more than 2.25 billion cups of steaming black heaven per day. Over 178,000,000 bags of coffee weighing 60 kilos apiece were exported last year, and countless millions work in cafes, roasteries and numerous other coffee-related businesses. As a titan of commerce coffee is a colossus.

And the very idea that we could lose coffee is reason enough to urgently revert back to donkeys and drive down carbon emissions.

"Arabica bean coffee represents around 60% of the world's coffee production," Davis explains. "But Arabica variety coffee is very sensitive to temperature and many other environmental factors. Because of this, increases in global temperature are adversely affecting production pretty much everywhere. Robusta, or *canephora* coffee accounts for about 40% of production, but doesn't possess the flavor of Arabica coffee."

There are 124 species of coffee known to science, most of them wild. Global climate change is adversely affecting as much as 60% of total coffee production, and we are in a race against time to do something about it.

Among wild species, there are a couple that could possibly replace Arabica coffee in areas where climate is causing decline in production. Davis and those with whom he works search jungles for wild coffee, and focus on species with large commercial potential, planning for a future that still includes the world's most beloved prepared beverage.

"Would you like a cup of coffee?" Of course I would. Aaron gets up from his chair and moves about, hovering over the various coffee appliances on tables in his office. He produces a small bag and tells me to hold out my hand. I do and he pours the tiniest coffee beans I have ever seen into my palm. "Sudan Rume," he tells me. As with all unroasted beans the green Sudan Rume has no particular aroma of note. But he has some roasted Rume, pouring some onto a small scale, and then into a burr grinder.

"How much coffee are you using per cup?"

"Nine point four five grams," he replies. Okay. We are in the coffee precision zone.

Soon water is boiled, and the freshly ground Sudan Rume is in an Aero Press used upside down. The small travel coffee maker is a favorite among aficionados and the method of using it upside down turns the device into an immersion coffee maker instead of a drip maker. Clever, very clever. When the coffee is finally done Aaron pours it into a glass cup and hands it to me. I take in the aroma, of fruits and flowers and wood, papaya, many notes parading before my nose. I take a taste. This is an amazing cup. When I return home I'll try to buy Sudan Rume online, to discover that a small bag costs about as much as a Tiffany egg, and you can't get any anyway.

Aaron and his colleagues have been working on coffee in the wild for many years, and they have found at least two wild species that may offer suitable substitutes for Arabica coffee. One species is *C. eugenoides*, which together with *C. canephora* coffee hybridized in Ethiopia in antiquity to form *C. Arabica*. This conjoining of species began somewhere between 350,000 – 610,000 years ago, according to genomic studies.

Another even more exciting species with commercial potential is *C. stenophylla.* which is native to Sierra Leone, Guinea, Liberia and Ivory Coast. "We're especially excited about *stenophylla*," he tells me. "We've grown some and roasted it, and in tastings 80% of the tasters thought it was Arabica."

There is the heart of the issue, the taste. Virtually all coffees can be roasted, ground and made into coffee. But many taste awful. Stenophylla, on the other hand, has the characteristics of a real coffee winner – productive, climate resistant, good tasting, nice aroma. After all, if coffee is going to sell, it has to taste good.

Canephora bean or robusta coffee is made into soluble coffee products like Nescafe'. It's truck stop coffee, with half the flavor and twice the caffeine of Arabica. It is blended into espresso blends and has gained in popularity in the coffee world. But *canephora* will never be the world's main bean, due to poor flavor in general.

154

So a newcomer species must pass the flavor bar or there is no point in the exercise of developing it commercially. And to pass muster among professional coffee tasters is no small matter. "I know tasters who can sip some coffee and tell you pretty much everything about it, including where it was grown." As gatekeepers of coffee, tasters can either elevate a coffee or condemn it. And if *C. stenophylla* passes muster among tasters, that is an excellent sign.

If Aaron Davis and his colleagues have it right, wild species of coffee including *C. Stenophylla* may replace Arabica bean coffee in many growing areas, providing a more stable crop that is resistant to higher temperatures and inconsistent water, while providing beans that satisfy coffee lovers. If all that works out, we'll continue drinking coffee, enjoying its majestic aroma and flavor and its wakeful stimulation.

Sign in a Massachusetts coffee shop

Chapter 21
An Urban Coffee Pilgrimage 2025

New York City runs on coffee. Walk down just about any avenue or street in Manhattan during the morning rush to work and you'll see at least one third of bustling pedestrians carrying sippy cups of coffee drinks. Drivers passing by hold cups in one hand and steer with the other. In taxi cabs you can espy large cups of coffee nestled in holders, visible above the dashboards.

According to various statistics I've read, approximately 14 million cups of coffee are drunk in the five New York City boroughs every day. That adds up to a super-caffeinated, coffee-charged culture, fueled by the hardest working bean on earth, the coffee bean.

When I travel to New York, which is mostly to appear on TV, I stay at the Warwick Hotel in midtown. It is comfortable and familiar and near Central Park. Any day after 5:00 a.m. I can walk out of the hotel, set off in any direction and find coffee in minutes. There is a Starbucks on every midtown corner (191 locations in NYC as of April 2025), plenty of independent coffee shops and small groceries and food trucks along the avenues, all serving steaming cups of hot coffee for early risers. On the fair days of summer or the harsh polar days of winter there is coffee.

Love of all things coffee has delivered me to New York City once again, this time to pay tribute to the city's most beloved beverage. I find myself patrolling an exhibition floor at the Jacob Javits Center at Coffee Fest, where New Yorker's love for coffee and voracious consumption of the beverage is given full and glorious expression.

Aisle after aisle of booths feature coffee companies, outfits who sell coffee accoutrements, companies who offer non-dairy coffee-lightening agents of all types, and even a latte' barista art contest. Can anyone make the Mona Lisa or the Empire State Building on the head of a latte'? Proficient latte' artists can make trees, flowers, and fanciful birds and animals with their skillful pouring of milk foam on the top of a latte'. As of yet there is no latte' art at the Metropolitan Museum but it is surely only a matter of time.

Latte art

Beware Coffee Fest convention-goer, for there is free espresso every few feet in every aisle, enough so that if you are not careful, you will be ripped to the eyeballs with caffeine within half an hour. People at all manner of coffee booths cheerfully offer free and delicious espressos as you go by. They woo you in with smiles and promises of a superior cup.

The booths are attractive, the aromas enchanting. The hissing of shiny espresso machines hard at work adds alluring atmosphere. Why not? One more can't hurt. Maybe even a double. You must carefully choose your free one and two shots. I've had about eight shots total, about six too many, and am done with more Joe for at least several hours, flying at 42,000 feet in an espresso jet stream. I am not alone. The free espressos are going like hotcakes. The room is lit up. After all, this is coffee we are talking about.

Dillanos Coffee booth

At Coffee Fest there are dozens of coffee exporters, several of them devoted to organically-produced beans, sustainable development and grower's cooperatives. At one booth a gigantic video of James Hoffmann, winner of the 2007 World Barista Championship and the current reigning guru of coffee, rises above the heads of visitors. A Coffee with Maca stand offers to awaken your senses.

Pastry companies display sweet baked treats for those shops who want to offer a little nosh to go with their coffee. The little individually-wrapped waffles are delicious. There is coffee with medicinal mushrooms, several tea companies, chai vendors, a booth called Post Brew selling mints to eliminate coffee breath, and fancy coffee making machinery.

Coffee with maca

Coffee guru James Hoffman looms over the crowd

I stop to ogle gleaming stainless steel Rancilio espresso machines, which at 900 – 5000 dollars apiece are unjustifiably costly if beautiful, for our kitchen. A man named James demonstrates a hi-tech Japanese coffee maker called Tiger Siphonysta, which looks like laboratory equipment and uses vacuum extraction to make what they promise is the perfect cup.

I run into my old friend Paul Wagner, whose company Noosh sells plant milk concentrates for those who want dairy alternatives. There are hats and t-shirts and bags for swag and an informative infographic demonstrating The Coffee Journey, from tree to cup. You can pick up free coffee stickers for your water bottles. Outstretched arms every few feet proffer more espresso for free. But I am not falling for that and will wait until my feet touch ground before tossing back any more.

Siphonysta coffee maker

At three different spots at Coffee Fest, seminars offer advice on perfect roasting, coffee making, and maximizing profits in a coffee shop. There are two seminars on the origins of coffee, and experts on coffee aroma and varieties from all over the world. Consultants offer their services to those who want to take their shops to the next level, whatever that may be.

Despite the occasional tea stand or bakery company, this event is about coffee, beloved coffee, majestic coffee, the beverage that rules much of the world and gets people going.

Coffee Seminar

As diverse and teeming as this convention might be, it represents only a wafer-thin segment of the world of coffee. All over the globe many millions of people are engaged in some manner with coffee, growing it, harvesting it, cranking out cups of drip coffee and espressos, drinking it, a multitude of activities. Coffee's reach is incalculably vast.

By mid-day the conventional hall is too packed and I see hundreds more people pouring through the entrance. These are adoring throngs. For many coffee is simply an essential part of the day. For others coffee is an object of ardor, even worship. Everyone here has paid good money to attend this, a total immersion into the stimulating and healthy drink that all but raises the dead. I take one final long stroll through the convention, knock back one more free double espresso in the last aisle and head for the door. Outside I glide 25 blocks back to my hotel, soaring on the refined and brilliant energy of the noble bean.

References

Alicandro   Tavani A, La Vecchia C. Coffee and cancer risk: a summary overview. Eur J Cancer Prev. 2017 Sep;26(5):424-432.

Alpini, Prospero https://en.wikipedia.org/wiki/Prospero_Alpini

Amiri R, Akbari M, Moradikor N. Bioactive potential and chemical compounds of coffee. Prog Brain Res. 2024;288:23-33.

Asuku AO, Ayinla MT, Olajide TS, Oyerinde TO, Yusuf JA, Bayo-Olugbami AA, Fajemidagba GA. Coffee and Parkinson's disease. Prog Brain Res. 2024;289:1-19.

Baba Budan https://www.coffeeam.com/pages/legend-baba-budan

Bae JH, Park JH, Im SS, Song DK. Coffee and health. Integr Med Res. 2014 Dec;3(4):189-191.

Bansal V, Chatterjee I. From bean to brain: Coffee, gray matter, and neuroprotection in neurological disorders spectrum. Prog Brain Res. 2024;289:169-180.

Bennet, Alan Weinberg, Bealer Bonnie K. The World of Caffeine, The Science and Culture of the World's Most Popular Drug. Routledge, 2002

Bidel S, Tuomilehto J. The Emerging Health Benefits of Coffee with an Emphasis on Type 2 Diabetes and Cardiovascular Disease. Eur Endocrinol. 2013 Aug;9(2):99-106.

Bonita JS, Mandarano M, Shuta D, Vinson J. Coffee and cardiovascular disease: in vitro, cellular, animal, and human studies. Pharmacol Res. 2007 Mar;55(3):187-98.

Bosso H, Barbalho SM, de Alvares Goulart R, Otoboni AMMB.

Green coffee: economic relevance and a systematic review of the effects on human health. Crit Rev Food Sci Nutr. 2023;63(3):394-410.

Chen Y, Zhang Y, Yang H, Ma Y, Zhou L, Lin J, Hou Y, Yu B, Wang Y. Association of Coffee and Tea Consumption with Cardiovascular Disease, Chronic Respiratory Disease, and their Comorbidity. Mol Nutr Food Res. 2022 Dec;66(24):e2200419.

Cheney, Ralph Holt. Coffee : a monograph of the economic species of the genus Coffea L. Literary Licensing LLC 2013

Chrysant SG. Coffee Consumption and Cardiovascular Health. Am J Cardiol. 2015 Sep 1;116(5):818-21.

Costa Rica Coffee Statistics https://www.fas.usda.gov/data/costa-rica-coffee-annual-9

Davis AP, Chadburn H, Moat J, O'Sullivan R, Hargreaves S, Nic Lughadha E. High extinction risk for wild coffee species and implications for coffee sector sustainability. Sci Adv. 2019 Jan 16;5(1):eaav3473.

de Melo Pereira GV, de Carvalho Neto DP, Magalhães Júnior AI, do Prado FG, Pagnoncelli MGB, Karp SG, Soccol CR. Chemical composition and health properties of coffee and coffee by-products. Adv Food Nutr Res. 2020;91:65-96.

Franz Georg Kolschitzky https://en.wikipedia.org/wiki/Jerzy_Franciszek_Kulczycki

Grosso G, Godos J, Galvano F, Giovannucci EL. Coffee, Caffeine, and Health Outcomes: An Umbrella Review. Annu Rev Nutr. 2017 Aug 21;37:131-156.

Haskell-Ramsay CF, Jackson PA, Forster JS, Dodd FL, Bowerbank SL, Kennedy DO. The Acute Effects of Caffeinated Black Coffee on Cognition and Mood in Healthy Young and Older Adults. Nutrients. 2018 Sep 30;10(10):1386.

Hayir Bey / Khair Bey https://en.wikipedia.org/wiki/Hayır_Bey

Hoffmann, James. The World Atlas of Coffee, Third Edition. Mitchell Beazley, 2022.

Italian Coffeehouses https://earthstoriez.com/history-and-evolution-of-the-coffeehouse-in-italy

Hawaii Coffee Statistics https://hdoa.hawaii.gov/wp-content/uploads/2022/08/Coffee-Stats-2021-2022-SOH-07.29.22r.pdf State of Hawaii Dept of Ag report 2021 2022

Iriondo-DeHond A, et al. Effects of Coffee and Its Components on the Gastrointestinal Tract and the Brain-Gut Axis. Nutrients. 2020 Dec 29;13(1):88.

Islam MT, et al. An Insight into the Therapeutic Potential of Major Coffee Components. Curr Drug Metab. 2018;19(6):544-556.

Ivory Coast Coffee Statistics https://www.ceicdata.com/en/ivory-coast/industrial-production/industrial-production-primary-sector-coffee

Jobin, Philippe The Coffees Produced Throughout The World. Philippe Jobin, 1992

Kennedy OJ, Roderick P, Buchanan R, Fallowfield JA, Hayes PC, Parkes J. Systematic review with meta-analysis: coffee consumption and the risk of cirrhosis. Aliment Pharmacol Ther. 2016 Mar;43(5):562-74.

Kikumura-Yano, Akemi, Azuma Elichiro, et al. The Kona Coffee Story: Along the Hawai'i Belt Road. Japanese American National Museum, 1995

Kim H, Kang SH, Kim SH, Kim SH, Hwang J, Kim JG, Han K, Kim JB. Drinking coffee enhances neurocognitive function by reorganizing brain functional connectivity. Sci Rep. 2021 Jul 13;11(1):14381.

Kobylińska, Z.; Biesiadecki, M.; Kuna, E.; Galiniak, S.; Mołoń, M. Coffee as a Source of Antioxidants and an Elixir of Youth. *Antioxidants* **2025**, *14*, 285.

Lewin, Lewis, M.D. Phantastica: A Classic Survey on the Use and Abuse of Mind Altering Plants. Park Street Press, 1998

Liang N, Kitts DD. Role of Chlorogenic Acids in Controlling Oxidative and Inflammatory Stress Conditions. Nutrients. 2015 Dec 25;8(1):16.

Lopes CR, Cunha RA. Impact of coffee intake on human aging: Epidemiology and cellular mechanisms. Ageing Res Rev. 2024 Dec;102:102581.

M Yelanchezian YM, Waldvogel HJ, Faull RLM, Kwakowsky A. Neuroprotective Effect of Caffeine in Alzheimer's Disease. Molecules. 2022 Jun 10;27(12):3737.

Mayer C, et al. Association between Coffee Consumption and Brain MRI Parameters in the Hamburg City Health Study. Nutrients. 2023 Jan 28;15(3):674.

Meamar M, Raise-Abdullahi P, Rashidy-Pour A, Raeis-Abdollahi E. Coffee and mental disorders: How caffeine affects anxiety and depression. Prog Brain Res. 2024;288:115-132.

Mendoza MF, Sulague RM, Posas-Mendoza T, Lavie CJ. Impact of Coffee Consumption on Cardiovascular Health. Ochsner J. 2023 Summer;23(2):152-158.

Murai T, Matsuda S. The Chemopreventive Effects of Chlorogenic Acids, Phenolic Compounds in Coffee, against Inflammation, Cancer, and Neurological Diseases. Molecules. 2023 Mar 4;28(5):2381.

Murata T, et al M. Suppression of Neuroinflammation by Coffee

Component Pyrocatechol via Inhibition of NF-κB in Microglia. Int J Mol Sci. 2023 Dec 25;25(1):316.

Nehlig A. Effects of coffee/caffeine on brain health and disease: What should I tell my patients? Pract Neurol. 2016 Apr;16(2):89-95.

Nguyen V, Taine EG, Meng D, Cui T, Tan W. Chlorogenic Acid: A Systematic Review on the Biological Functions, Mechanistic Actions, and Therapeutic Potentials. Nutrients. 2024 Mar 23;16(7):924.

O'Keefe JH, et al. Effects of habitual coffee consumption on cardiometabolic disease, cardiovascular health, and all-cause mortality. J Am Coll Cardiol. 2013 Sep 17;62(12):1043-1051.

O'Keefe JH, DiNicolantonio JJ, Lavie CJ. Coffee for Cardioprotection and Longevity. Prog Cardiovasc Dis. 2018 May-Jun;61(1):38-42.

Ősz BE, Jîtcă G, Ştefănescu RE, Puşcaş A, Tero-Vescan A, Vari CE. Caffeine and Its Antioxidant Properties-It Is All about Dose and Source. Int J Mol Sci. 2022 Oct 28;23(21):13074.

Paiva C, Beserra B, Reis C, Dorea JG, Da Costa T, Amato AA. Consumption of coffee or caffeine and serum concentration of inflammatory markers: A systematic review. Crit Rev Food Sci Nutr. 2019;59(4):652-663.

Paz-Graniel I, et al; PREDIMED-Plus Investigators. Association between coffee consumption and total dietary caffeine intake with cognitive functioning: cross-sectional assessment in an elderly Mediterranean population. Eur J Nutr. 2021 Aug;60(5):2381-2396.

Pendergrast, Mark. Uncommon Grounds: The History of Coffee and How It Transformed Our World. Basic Books, 1999

Peruvian Coffee Statistics

https://apps.fas.usda.gov/newgainapi/api/Report/DownloadReportByFileName?fileName=Coffee+Annual_Lima_Peru_PE2025-0018.pdf

Rai SP, Ansari AH, Singh D, Singh S. Coffee, antioxidants, and brain inflammation. Prog Brain Res. 2024;289:123-150.

Raise-Abdullahi P, Raeis-Abdollahi E, Meamar M, Rashidy-Pour A. Effects of coffee on cognitive function. Prog Brain Res. 2024;288:133-166.

Rauwolf, Leonhard
https://en.wikipedia.org/wiki/Leonhard_Rauwolf

Raza ML, Haghipanah M, Moradikor N. Coffee and stress management: How does coffee affect the stress response? Prog Brain Res. 2024;288:59-80.

Raza ML. Coffee and brain health: An introductory overview. Prog Brain Res. 2024;288:1-22.

Rebello SA, van Dam RM. Coffee consumption and cardiovascular health: getting to the heart of the matter. Curr Cardiol Rep. 2013 Oct;15(10):403.

Safe S, Kothari J, Hailemariam A, Upadhyay S, Davidson LA, Chapkin RS. Health Benefits of Coffee Consumption for Cancer and Other Diseases and Mechanisms of Action. Int J Mol Sci. 2023 Jan 31;24(3):2706.

Salojärvi, J., Rambani, A., Yu, Z. *et al.* The genome and population genomics of allopolyploid *Coffea arabica* reveal the diversification history of modern coffee cultivars. *Nat Genet* **56**, 721–731 (2024).

Schivelbusch, Wolfgang. Tastes of Paradise. Vintage Books, 1993

Socała K, Szopa A, Serefko A, Poleszak E, Wlaź P.

Neuroprotective Effects of Coffee Bioactive Compounds: A Review. Int J Mol Sci. 2020 Dec 24;22(1):107.

Spiller, G.A. (1998). Caffeine (1st ed.). CRC Press. https://doi.org/10.1201/9780429126789

A, La Vecchia C. Coffee and cancer: a review of epidemiological studies, 1990-1999. Eur J Cancer Prev. 2000 Aug;9(4):241-56.

Turnbull D, Rodricks JV, Mariano GF, Chowdhury F. Caffeine and cardiovascular health. Regul Toxicol Pharmacol. 2017 Oct;89:165-185.

Unno K, Taguchi K, Hase T, Meguro S, Nakamura Y. Coffee Polyphenol, Chlorogenic Acid, Suppresses Brain Aging and Its Effects Are Enhanced by Milk Fat Globule Membrane Components. Int J Mol Sci. 2022 May 23;23(10):5832.

Valdeir Viana Freitas, et al. Coffee: A comprehensive overview of origin, market, and the quality process, Trends in Food Science & Technology, Volume 146, 2024

Vietnam Coffee Statistics
https://apps.fas.usda.gov/newgainapi/api/Report/DownloadReportByFileName?fileName=Coffee%20Semi-annual_Hanoi_Vietnam_VM2024-0047.pdf

Vietnam development
https://www.nestle.com/sites/default/files/asset library/documents/reports/csv%20reports/agriculture%20and%20 rural%20development/robust_production_vietnam.pdf

Vietnam coffee varieties
https://vietnamagriculture.nongnghiep.vn/wasis-great-contribution-to-the-coffee-industry-transferring-high-quality-coffee-varieties-for-replanting-d400144.html

von Bibra, Baron Ernst. Plant Intoxicants. Park Street Press, 1995

Wasim S, Kukkar V, Awad VM, Sakhamuru S, Malik BH.

Neuroprotective and Neurodegenerative Aspects of Coffee and Its Active Ingredients in View of Scientific Literature. Cureus. 2020 Aug 5;12(8):e9578.

Ye Y, Zhong R, Xiong XM, Wang CE. Association of coffee intake with bone mineral density: a Mendelian randomization study. Front Endocrinol (Lausanne). 2024 Mar 20;15:1328748.

You DC, Kim YS, Ha AW, Lee YN, Kim SM, Kim CH, Lee SH, Choi D, Lee JM. Possible health effects of caffeinated coffee consumption on Alzheimer's disease and cardiovascular disease. Toxicol Res. 2011 Mar;27(1):7-10.

Youngyo Kim, Youjin Je, Edward Giovannucci Eur J Epidemiol. 2019 Aug;34(8):731-752.doi: 10.1007/s10654-019-00524-3. Epub 2019 May 4.Coffee consumption and all-cause and cause-specific mortality: a meta-analysis by potential modifiers

Yuan S, Carter P, Mason AM, Burgess S, Larsson SC. Coffee Consumption and Cardiovascular Diseases: A Mendelian Randomization Study. Nutrients. 2021 Jun 28;13(7):2218.

Zhang Y, Yang H, Li S, Li WD, Wang Y. Consumption of coffee and tea and risk of developing stroke, dementia, and poststroke dementia: A cohort study in the UK Biobank. PLoS Med. 2021 Nov 16;18(11):e1003830.

Zhao LG, Li ZY, et al. Coffee drinking and cancer risk: an umbrella review of meta-analyses of observational studies. BMC Cancer. 2020 Feb 5;20(1):101.